Colleen Wise

Casting Shadows

Creating Visual Dimension in Your Quilts

C&T PUBLISHING

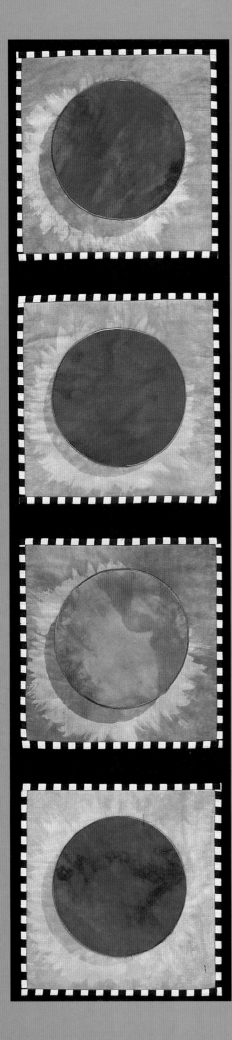

Text ©2005 Colleen Wise
Artwork ©2005 C&T Publishing

Publisher: AMY MARSON

Editorial Director: GAILEN RUNGE

Acquisitions Editor: JAN GRIGSBY

Editor: LIZ ANELOSKI

Technical Editors: RENE STEINPRESS, JOYCE LYTLE

Copyeditor/Proofreader: WORDFIRM INC.

Cover Designer: KRISTEN YENCHE

Design Director/Book Designer: ROSE SHEIFER

Illustrator: RICHARD SHEPPARD

Production Assistant: MATT ALLEN

Photography: LUKE MULKS and DIANE PEDERSEN, unless otherwise noted

Published by C&T Publishing, Inc., P.O. Box 1456, Lafayette, California, 94549

Front cover: *Emerald City* by Colleen Wise

Back cover: *Botanica*, *Square Peg*, *Round Hole*, and *Corona*, by Colleen Wise

Library of Congress Cataloging-in-Publication Data

Wise, Colleen,

Casting shadows : creating visual dimension in your quilts / Colleen Wise.
    p. cm.
Includes index.
ISBN 987-1-57120-295-6 (paper trade)
ISBN 1-57120-295-1 (paper trade)
1. Patchwork—Patterns. 2. Quilting—Patterns. 3. Appliqué—Patterns.
I. Title.

TT835.W556 2005

746.46—dc22

2004025866

Printed in China
10 9 8 7 6 5 4 3

Dedication

To my family

Acknowledgments

In 1991, my mother, Arlene Wise, introduced me to quilting and changed my life. We borrowed a sewing machine from a neighbor, un-cobwebbed the iron, and cut up some old shirts to put together that first Log Cabin block. But the lessons I've learned from her go far beyond quilting. Mom, for everything you have done and everything you are—thank you.

For all the amazing quilting teachers I've had through the years, beginning with Jeanne Steinhorst, Nan Naubert, and Marti Carroll—thank you for your enthusiasm and inspiration. You'll never know what sparks you have started.

Everyone should have a circle of friends like this—the Wild Wednesday Women meet every week (guess which day) and share quilting ideas, creativity, art, dreams, and life in general. Thanks for being there, always—Barb Sherrill, Debi Harney, Ellen Koehn, Linda Rudin Frizzell, Susan Harris, and Kim McCloskey. See you on, well, Thursday.

For Evie Griffin, who took a chance on an unknown commodity way back when and hired me to teach at her shop, the Quilt Barn, and for all the shop owners, especially Pam Hewitt and Liz Warner, who have encouraged me along the way—thank you. Support your local quilt shop.

And for the people I live with, who put up with pins in the couch and threads on their clothes and love me anyway—thanks Allan, Cameron, Hannah, and Abby. I love you too.

CONTENTS

Introduction

We live in a world of three dimensions, and as quilt artists, we create in a world of two dimensions. Let's change that. Let's open up our work to the possibility of another dimension.

I have been exploring the use of shadows in my work to imply a sense of depth. Leaves, circles, and other shapes seem to hover just off the surface of the quilt. Circles become spheres; spheres bounce or float. The viewer is drawn deep into the depths of the quilt. Space is relative here.

Our minds are enchanted with the illusion of the dimensional. We want to reach out and touch it, verify that it truly is an illusion and not actually defying the laws of gravity.

The techniques I've developed are easy, fun, and effective. Some are simple and familiar: piecing, appliqué, fusing, quilting. Others may be new to you: surface design using discharge, paint, or oil sticks.

As in any endeavor, it pays to have plenty of tools in your tool belt before you start working. These techniques are just that: tools to help you create the vision you see in your mind.

In my opinion, the Pacific Northwest is one of the most beautiful places on Earth, especially western Washington State, where I live. Snowcapped Mount Rainier looms over my backyard, and the beach is only a few miles away. Winters are mild, and summers are cool. Everything thrives here; gardening is a joy. We have it all—including the *rain*.

We are famous for our rain. And yet it really isn't the rain that drags most people down—it's the cloudiness. For much of the year, there is a perpetual low ceiling of heavy gray overcast. Sometimes I long to see blue sky and sunshine . . . and shadows.

Shadows suffer from a bad reputation. They always seem sinister, or at least mysterious. But there is great rejoicing in the Northwest whenever we see shadows because it can mean only one thing: The sun is shining!

So I like to include shadows in my work. I love playing with three dimensions, and using shadows allows me to create a sense of depth in my quilts. When I add shadows, objects appear to float off the surface of the quilt. And the best part is that by adding shadows in my work, I'm not adding darkness. I am actually adding *light*!

TOOLS AND TECHNIQUES

I have a variety of tools in my tool belt that I use to add dimension to my work:

- Color and value
- Piecing
- Appliqué (hand, machine, fusible)
- Dyeing and discharging
- Painting
- Quilting

I will basically use any and every tool I need to achieve the look I want in a certain piece. Each of these techniques is effective alone. But I often use more than one technique in any given quilt. None of them is difficult, and any of them can add a fresh new look to your quilting, whether you are a traditional quilter or an innovative artist.

But before we dig into the nuts and bolts of techniques, let's spend a little time thinking about shadows. First, a disclaimer, though: I am a nerd, a geek, a total pointy-headed intellectual type. I love math and physics. I love thinking about things like how shadows appear to us and how the distance and orientation from both the viewer and the light source affect the direction and shape of the shadows we see. I want to take you on a journey through my thought process. Come on—it's fun and easy!

Sometimes . . .

Photo: Allan Maas

Most of the time . . .

Photo: Colleen Wise

. . .there is great rejoicing in the Northwest whenever we see shadows because it can mean only one thing: The sun is shining!

The viewer is close to the leaf, and the sun is overhead; the shadow is narrow.

The sun is a little lower in the sky; more of the shadow is visible.

The sun is lower yet; the shadow is separate from the leaf itself.

PROPERTIES OF SHADOWS

Let's think about shadows and what they look like. The *color, shape,* and *orientation* of an object's shadow influence how we perceive that object in space. Shadows also give us clues about the distance from and location of the *light source,* as well as information about the *object* that casts the shadow. The shape of the shadow may be the same as the shape of the object itself, or it may be lengthened or distorted. The shadow may appear directly below an object or off to one side, depending on the location of the light source and the perspective of the viewer. The shadows cast by the sun are different from those cast by a streetlight . . . or by a desk lamp. How these ideas are handled contributes to the success of the optical illusion in your quilt.

The Orientation of Shadows

Picture this: A leaf is floating on the surface of a shallow pool of clear water at high noon on a sunny day. You are wading in this little pool looking down at the floating leaf. You can see the shadow of the leaf on the bottom of the pool.

The shadow will be located directly below the leaf. That's because the sun is directly overhead at high noon. If you are wading in the water very close to the leaf, you will see just a sliver of shadow along the edge of the leaf that is closest to you. As the sun starts to go down, you will see more and more of the shadow. The water may be just deep enough that the shadow appears completely separate from the leaf itself—they don't even touch. You and the leaf haven't moved; the light source has, and it has moved the shadow too, from your perspective.

Seeing a shadow along the edge of a leaf convinces us that the leaf is floating. We can harness the power of that illusion. By adding a shadow along the edge of blocks or objects in our quilts, we can make them float too!

Shadows tell us about the direction of the light source because shadows always fall away from the light. By controlling the orientation of shadows in a quilt, we also control the perception of where the light source is. What are our options?

A Place to Start

Place the sun on the right.

Below is a traditional block-based quilt. The blocks are "floating" and casting shadows on the background of the quilt. The light source appears to be in the upper right corner of the quilt.

Move the sun from the right to the left.

To move the sun to the left instead of the right, just put the shadows on the right sides of the blocks instead of the left.

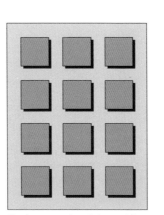

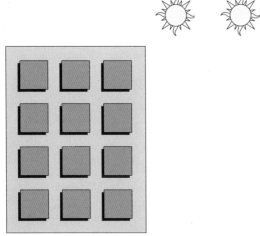

Shadows on the left and bottom sides of the quilt blocks imply a light source that is toward the upper right corner of the quilt.

Shadows on the right and bottom sides of the quilt blocks imply a light source that is toward the upper left corner of the quilt.

WISE TIP When I am deciding in which direction my shadows will fall, I usually think about where my finished quilt will be hanging. If there is a window to one side of the quilt, I will create shadows that fall away from the window to create the illusion that the light from the window is the light source that is casting the shadows on the quilt.

Allow the sun to rise or set.

To move the light source vertically in the sky (either more like noon or more like late afternoon), make your shadows narrower or wider.

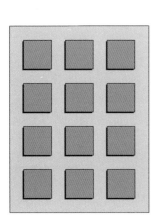

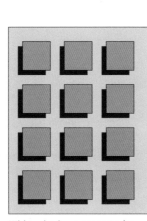

Narrow shadows imply a light source that is nearly overhead, like the sun at noon.

Wider shadows seem to be cast by a lower light source, like the sun in late afternoon.

Move the sun to a different angle.

To move the light source to a different angle, make the shadows asymmetrical.

When shadows along the bottom and side of each block are the same width, the sun appears to be above the top corner of the quilt—at a 45° angle. Adjusting the width of the vertical and horizontal shadows independently changes the angle of the quilt to the sun.

Narrow vertical shadows paired with wide horizontal shadows put the sun nearer to the top of the quilt.

Wide vertical shadows paired with narrow horizontal shadows put the sun nearer to the side of the quilt.

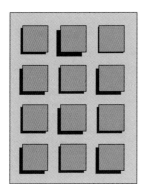

Varying the width of each block's shadow makes the blocks appear to be floating at different heights. Blocks can be lined up by block edges . . .

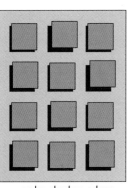

. . . or by shadow edges.

Float the blocks at different heights.

To float your blocks at different elevations above the surface of the background, add shadows that vary in width in an unpredictable but logical manner.

The wider the shadow, the higher that particular block appears to be floating; the narrower the shadow, the closer to the ground. The vertical and horizontal shadows should be the same width within any given block; they vary only from block to block.

Logic is the key.

Whatever you do, have a reason for the orientation and size of your shadows to make the most convincing three-dimensional illusion.

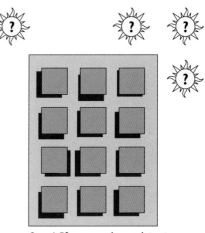

Oops! If you are inconsistent with your shadows, the illusion is lost. The direction of the light source is not clear.

THE SHAPE OF SHADOWS

Let's go back to the pool. Picture that leaf again, the one that's floating in the shallow pool of clear water at high noon on a sunny day (page 8). There you still are, wading in this little pool looking at the floating leaf. This time, let's look at the *shape* of the leaf's shadow on the bottom of the pool.

The shape of the shadow will be the same as the shape of the leaf itself. That's because the sun is directly overhead. As the sun sinks lower, the shape of the shadow will slowly change; it will stretch and elongate as the sun goes down. The shadow will become more and more distorted as the sun nears the horizon. We've all seen this in late afternoon, when we cast long, impossibly slender shadows of ourselves. The angle of the light source makes a difference in the way a shadow appears.

Distorted and Puddled Shadows

Sometimes shadows don't look very much like the object that is casting the shadow. A leaf floating on a pool casts a shadow that looks like a leaf, but a tree in a lawn casts a shadow that doesn't look very much like a tree. It looks like a puddle under the tree. Let's consider these kinds of shadows.

We can distort shadows in two ways: by moving the viewer and by moving the light source. If the direction of light source changes, the shadows that it casts can be distorted, like your shadow in the late afternoon. Likewise, if we move away from the object that is casting the shadow, the shape of the shadow will look different to us. We can use this knowledge for different effects.

Let's say we have a nice bouncy ball. The ball is sitting on the driveway at high noon and the sun is shining. Its shadow is a blurry circle. If we stand very close to the ball and look down on it, we can see that the shadow is a circle. But if we back away from the ball, the shadow starts to flatten out and look more like an oval and less like a circle. The farther away we go, the more flattened the oval becomes. And if we lie on the ground, the shadow will be such a flat oval that it will almost look like a blurry line. You can't tell that the shadow is a circle at all. I call these "puddled shadows."

Puddled shadows are easy and fun. They add a nice dimension to appliqué. Adding a puddled shadow to an appliquéd piece implies that the object casting the shadow is three-dimensional. Puddled shadows can be discharged, painted, or appliquéd. The vague shape of puddled shadows has another benefit: for artistically impaired people like me, they are easy to draw!

In the quilt *Fruits of the Spirit* (page 97), each circle has a puddled shadow underneath it to imply that there is a third dimension; the shadows are an attempt to convince you that the flat circles are actually spheres. All the puddled shadows are the same shape and distance from the circles. This gives the impression that the spheres are floating at an equal distance from the ground.

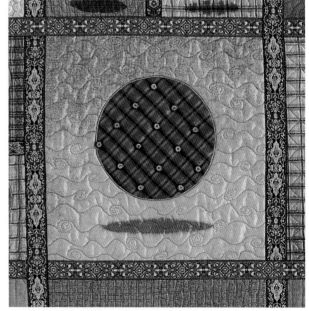

Fruits of the Spirit detail (full quilt page 97)

Now look at this quilt, *Gravity*. It's very similar in design to *Fruits of the Spirit* (page 97), except the shadows are not as consistent. Each ball has a puddled shadow underneath it, just as in *Fruits of the Spirit*. But the balls are arranged so that the top row appears to be resting on the ground, and each successive row of balls bounces higher and higher. It's the placement of each ball relative to its shadow that creates this illusion. The balls in the top row appear to be resting on the ground because the bottom edge of each ball rests in the center of its oval puddled shadow. As your eye moves down the quilt, the balls don't touch their shadows at all. Each row of balls appears to be bouncing higher than the row above it, because the balls are placed higher and higher above their puddled shadows. The oval shadows become more flattened and thin as the balls bounce higher. The greater the distance between the ball and its shadow, the higher the bounce!

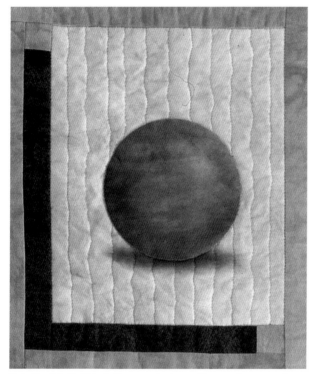

Gravity detail. This ball seems to be resting on the ground.

Gravity detail. But this one is bouncing!

Nearby Light Sources

So far we've been thinking about a rather large and powerful light source—the sun. But remember, I live in the Pacific Northwest, so my light source is far more likely to be something like a desk lamp than the sun. How does the relative *distance* of the light source affect the shape and orientation of shadows?

Back to that pool one more time. Let's say that there are actually a lot of leaves floating on the surface. They are all casting shadows at the same angle because the light source (the sun) is so very far away. The distance between the leaves and the bottom of the pool is nothing compared to the distance between the leaves and the sun.

Suppose we move that pool into my studio (don't try this at home!). Instead of being lit by the sun, the pool is now lit by a desk lamp near the surface of the water at one end of the pool. We'll float near the ceiling of my studio, looking straight down at the leaves. When we turn on that lamp and point it at the leaves on the pool, we can see that the width and direction of the shadows depend on the distance and direction of each leaf from the light source.

The leaf that is closest to the lamp has a shadow that is narrow and close to the leaf. Shadows lengthen and stretch as your eye moves away from the lamp. The leaves that are far from the lamp cast long shadows that stretch farther away from their leaves, like shadows in late afternoon.

If we were to incorporate the idea of a nearby light source into a quilt, we would add shadows that lengthen as your eye moves across the piece. Shadows would change width in a predictable manner, lengthening as you move farther away from the light source.

You can see this effect in the quilt *Amish Weave* (page 24). I placed that imaginary desk lamp at the upper right hand corner of the quilt. The shadows lengthen as your eye moves diagonally across the quilt. You can see the shadows widen as you move from the very narrow shadows in the upper right corner to the very wide shadows in the lower left. The colorful woven pattern seems to float above the surface of the background at a constant elevation, but the lengthening shadows make it feel as if the light source is very close to the upper right corner of the quilt. Grading the value of the background from lightest (in the upper right corner, where you expect the desk lamp to be) to darkest (in the lower left corner, far from the lamp) adds to this illusion.

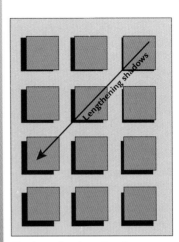

Shadows that lengthen in a predictable way as you move diagonally across the surface of the quilt create a sense of a nearby light source at the corner of the quilt.

WISE TIP If all this perspective makes your head hurt, don't strain anything! You can always make your shadows even and consistent in terms of shape, color, and orientation and still get a fabulous three-dimensional effect.

Amish Weave detail. The shadows are narrow near the "light."

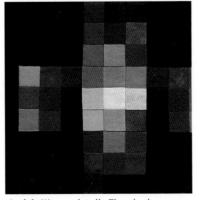

Amish Weave detail. The shadows are wide far from the "light."

THE COLOR OF SHADOWS

Picture that leaf again, the one that's floating in the shallow pool of clear water at high noon on a sunny day. There you still are, standing on the edge of this little pool, looking at the floating leaf. This time, let's look at the *color* of the leaf's shadow on the bottom of the pool.

The leaf may be green, brown, or screaming-purple-polka-dot; it doesn't matter. Look at its shadow instead. The shadow itself is . . . what color? You might think "black," but that's not necessarily true. Look carefully. The color is a darker, grayer version of the color of the bottom of the pool. If the bottom of the pool is muddy brown, the shadow may appear black. But if the pool is the shallow water of a clean, white, sandy beach in Tahiti, the shadow will be a dark beige or grayish color, like dark sand. If it's an aqua-painted toddler pool at the local municipal pool, the shadow will be dark, dull aqua. And if it's a puddle in your nice green lawn because you forgot to turn off the sprinkler, the shadow will be a dark, dull green.

Photo: Colleen Wise

The color of the shadow depends on the color of the background, not on the color of the object itself.

The same principle applies to choosing a "shadow color" in a quilt. The color of the shadow relates to the color of the background, not to the colors of the objects that are "floating." The floating objects can be individual things on your quilt, such as leaves or circles or abstract shapes, each with its own shadow; or the floating objects can be entire quilt blocks, floating above the background of sashing and border. The principle about shadow color is the same in both cases. *The shadow color relates to the color of the background of the quilt, not to the colors of the floating objects or the floating quilt blocks.*

For example, suppose you are a traditional quilter and you have decided to "float" your traditional blocks in a slightly nontraditional way, as you will see in Chapter 4. You plan to "shadow" your blocks in a pieced setting with sashing and a border. You choose one fabric to use for both your sashing and your border, and at the same time, you choose a different fabric for your shadow. The color of the shadow fabric will relate to the sashing/border fabric, not to the fabrics in your traditional blocks. So, if your blocks are, for example, shades of soft, soothing browns and golds, and you have decided on a nice beige for the sashing and border, your shadow fabric should be a darker, duller shade of the beige. If your blocks are done up in wild novelty prints in neon colors, and you have decided to use the same nice beige for your sashing and border to calm those colors, your shadow fabric is . . . the same darker, duller shade of beige as in the previous quilt. It doesn't matter what color your blocks are. The shadow color relates to the color of the background—in this case, the beige sashing/border fabric.

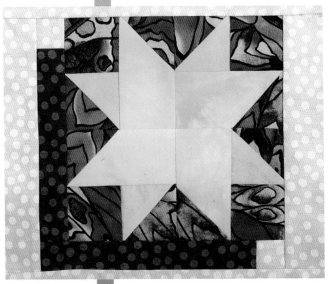

The color of the blocks doesn't matter. The shadow color relates to the color of the background.

Pure colors do not make very convincing shadows. Perhaps your background is a pale grayish blue. Bright royal blue may be darker in value, but it won't make a very convincing shadow. Shadows tend to be dull, grayed-down colors.

This color is too "pure" to be a convincing shadow.

This grayer color is better.

The shadow fabric should match the background in texture and scale.

It bears repeating: The shadow fabric should be a darker, duller shade of the *background* color.

Shadow fabric should also match the background fabric in texture and scale. If you have a small calico-type background, a swirly hand-dyed fabric may not make the best shadow. A darker, grayer small calico print might be a better choice. If you have a busy print for a background, you can also use a darker and duller (but still busy) print for a shadow. Or you may decide it looks too busy and needs a solid charcoal gray or black to better define the shadows.

I like to buy (or dye) my background and shadow fabrics at the same time. Sometimes a manufacturer will produce a fabric line in just the right colorways, so that I can choose one fabric for my background and find the very same print in a darker, duller color for the shadow. That makes it easy!

Easy choices!

I always audition my fabric choices before I make a decision. If I have blocks, I lay a block on the background fabric with just a half-inch sliver of shadow fabric peeking out along the bottom and one side of the block. Then I stand back and have a look (a reducing lens is very helpful here). Does this fabric convince me that the block is casting a shadow on the background? I look at it very critically. Is the shadow too dark, too bold, too pure in color, too light? Is my eye drawn to the shadow, or does the shadow even fail to register? If all I see is the shadow fabric, I should step down to something a little less strong; it's either too dark or too intense in color. If the shadow fabric is too light, I may wonder why my blocks don't seem to float. The shadows are fading into the background. I should try something a little darker.

Shadow fabric is too intense.

Shadow fabric is too light.

Shadow fabric is just right!

I always audition my fabric choices before I make a decision. . . . Does this fabric convince me that the block is casting a shadow on the background?

Shadows should be a darker, duller, grayer shade of the background fabric. Having said all that, if you are struggling with the concept, or you just can't find the right fabric, well, then, you can always try black or charcoal gray. Think of them as insurance . . . there if you need them.

If I don't have ready-made blocks to take to the quilt shop (either because I'll be appliquéing objects directly onto the background, or because I haven't made the blocks yet . . . or because I am just fabric shopping for fun!), I will audition fabrics by laying them together, with the shadow fabric just peeking out from under the background fabric. I've been known to prop up the bolt of potential background fabric, with the bolt of shadow fabric peeking out from behind it, and step back across the shop and squint. And I ask myself: Does it work?

Does this work?

When we place shadows behind objects on our quilts, we control the color, shape, and orientation of those shadows. And our choices influence the perception of the viewer. The viewer does not have the luxury of watching the shadows on your quilt change appearance over time, as we do with a leaf floating on a pool. Time is frozen. It's just an illusion—one that we, as the artists, get to control.

Now that we have thought so hard about shadows, let's apply our new knowledge to the nuts and bolts of quilting design. It's time to put some tools in our tool belts.

Chapter Two

COLOR

Most quilters adore color. It's one of our very favorite things about quilting, isn't it? Choosing colors for a new quilt can be the most creative, fun, and agonizing process in quilting. Nothing is quite as satisfying as pulling colors together, standing back, and just drinking in all that color. Personally, I use color as an antidote to our gray Northwest winter days. There's nothing like some vivid hand-dyed fabrics on the design wall to lift the spirits!

We don't need to have a degree in art to understand the impact of color, but a tiny little bit of color theory will help us understand how to use color more effectively. Let's start with some definitions:

- A pure color is a *hue*.

- If you add white to a hue, you create a *tint*. Pastels are tints. Tints are lighter than the original hue.

- If you add black to a hue, you create a *shade*. Shades are darker than the original hue.

- If you add gray to a hue, you create a *tone*. Tones can be lighter or darker than the original, but a tone is not as "pure" a color as the original—it is grayed down, dampened down, softer, duller, more neutral than the original.

Color and value have been used for ages to create a sense of depth in all kinds of art. Let's consider color and value as they apply to quilting and see how we can use them to create a sense of depth in our quilts.

But first, how do we define color, and what on earth is value?

A color card from *3-in-1 Color Tool* showing a pure color and its tints, shades, and tones

Using Color to Create Depth

When you stop at a scenic overlook and look out at a beautiful view, color affects how you perceive the scene. The colors in the foreground tend to be more intense, dark, and pure. As you look out toward the horizon, the colors fade and begin to gray out; that is, they become paler, less like pure hues, and more like tones. The distant colors are literally "toned down."

Photo: Allan Maas

Distant colors fade and gray out.

We can use color to imply distance when we create landscape quilts. Our foreground colors should be intense and pure. Colors in the distance are lighter and grayer tones than the foreground. You can see a good example of this in Barb Sherrill's landscape quilt *Wild Rhodies*.

Wild Rhodies by Barb Sherrill, Graham, Washington, 25" x 31", 2004. The colors are strong in the foreground and fade in the distance.

We can also use color in a more subtle way to connote depth, by playing with the temperature of the color. Cool colors—blues, greens, purples—tend to recede visually, to become the background. Warm colors—reds, yellows, oranges—tend to advance; they pop right out at you. Using warm colors in strategic places can make those colors appear to be closer to you. Save your cool colors for background.

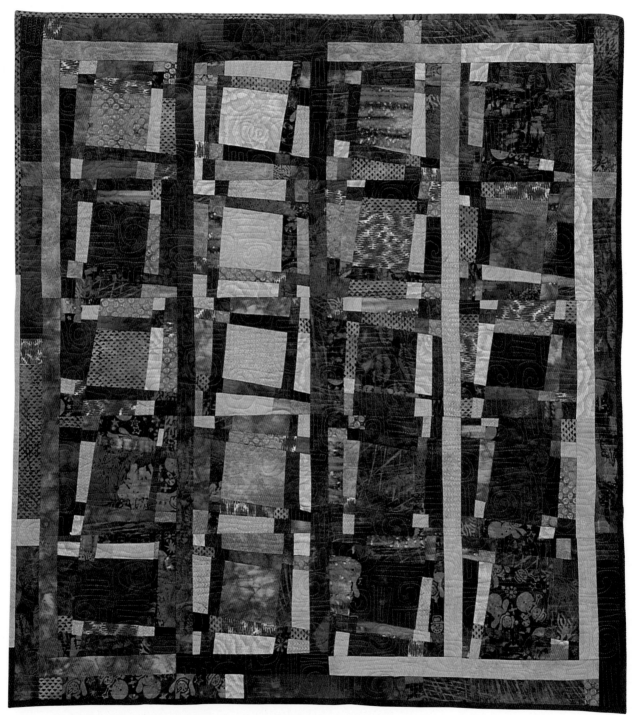

Arles by Debi Harney, Puyallup, Washington, 46" x 42", 2004. Pattern: *Sticks and Stones* by Barb's Elegant Designs. The warm colors pop right out at you.

VALUE

Value is the relative lightness or darkness of a color. We love working with color, but it's really not the most important thing. In quilting, *value* is actually more important than color. And value can be more of a struggle, less of a joy, than color. Value is not difficult; it's just not as glamorous as color. But when it comes to quilting, develop an eye for value.

Value is separate from color. It allows us to compare colors, to decide which is darker—this red or this green?—without being distracted by the colors themselves. If you have seen black-and-white movies, television, or photos, you know what value is. When you take the color out of the picture, it's all shades of gray. It doesn't matter if the colors are pure hues, tints, shades, or tones. They are either darker or lighter than the colors around them. That's *value*.

Value is relative. It depends on what's around it. A medium-value fabric may be considered "dark" when it is put next to pastels. Or it may be treated as a "light" if all the other colors with it are of darker value. There are only two colors with absolute value; that is, there are only two colors about which you can *always* say "this is dark" or "this is light" and be correct. Those colors are black and white. Everything else is relative.

How can we determine value? There are some tricks and tools that can help.

■ Looking through a red or green filter (sometimes called a "value finder") can help.

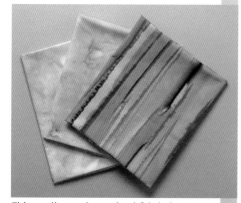

This medium-value striped fabric becomes a dark when it is paired with lighter values.

The same fabric becomes a light when it is paired with darker values.

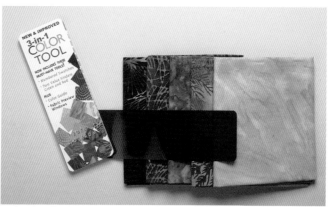

Red value finder

Green value finder

Sometimes distance makes value more apparent. A reducing lens makes things look far away. If you don't have a reducing lens (or a door peephole, or a wide-angle lens on your camera, or the back end of a pair of binoculars), you can always just step back and squint.

Reducing lenses

Getting a black-and-white image is a great way to determine value—you can photocopy your fabrics, or take a black-and-white photo of them. Some digital cameras can take black-and-white photos as well as color.

A photocopy can help you determine value.

You can also turn off the color in your own eyes. Wait until your eyes have adjusted to darkness and then view the fabric in very low light, like just before dawn. If you're not a morning person, pull the shades and simulate dawn by previewing your fabrics in very low light conditions.

. . . There are only two colors with absolute value; that is, there are only two colors about which you can always say "this is dark" or "this is light" and be correct. Those colors are black and white. Everything else is relative.

In Chapter 1, we discussed the color of shadows and concluded that shadows are a darker, duller shade of the background color. Now we can put this concept in more technical terms: Shadows are a *tone* of *darker value* than the background color.

Using Value to Create Depth

Quilters have used value to create three-dimensional effects for years. Consider the traditional Baby Blocks or Tumbling Blocks quilt; it looks like three-dimensional cubes stacked on top of each other. The pattern is really only diamonds sewn together, but by placing three different values (light, medium, and dark) in a specific pattern, the illusion of three-dimensional blocks appears. Note that color is not as important as value. The illusion works even when the colors don't match.

In *Bob and Weave* (page 26), I've used value and color together to create the illusion of ribbons that weave over and under each other. The piecing is simple, but if you pay careful attention to value, a more complicated pattern emerges. The ribbons maintain their color throughout their length; that is, the red ribbon stays red all the way across the quilt. The only thing that changes is the value of the red, in five steps from light to dark.

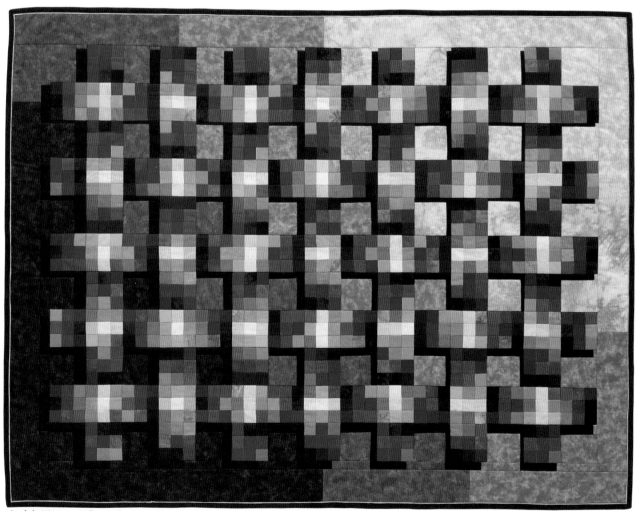

Amish Weave, 42" x 55"

Compare *Bob and Weave* to the quilt *Amish Weave*. It is a similar pattern to *Bob and Weave*, just slightly expanded. In *Amish Weave*, I have completely disregarded color. I've focused only on value. The illusion of weaving over and under still works! Proof that value is more important than color.

Linda Bennington Devereaux's quilt *Stuff It* eliminates color altogether and uses only value to create a sense of depth.

Color and value are great tools to have in your toolbox. Think about them as you design and plan your next quilt. You may be able to incorporate a little dimension in your piece!

Stuff It by Linda Bennington Devereaux, Lakewood, Washington, 79" x 79", 2001

Bob and Weave

Bands of color appear to weave over and under each other in this easy three-dimensional-looking quilt. Paying careful attention to value will make the illusion appear.

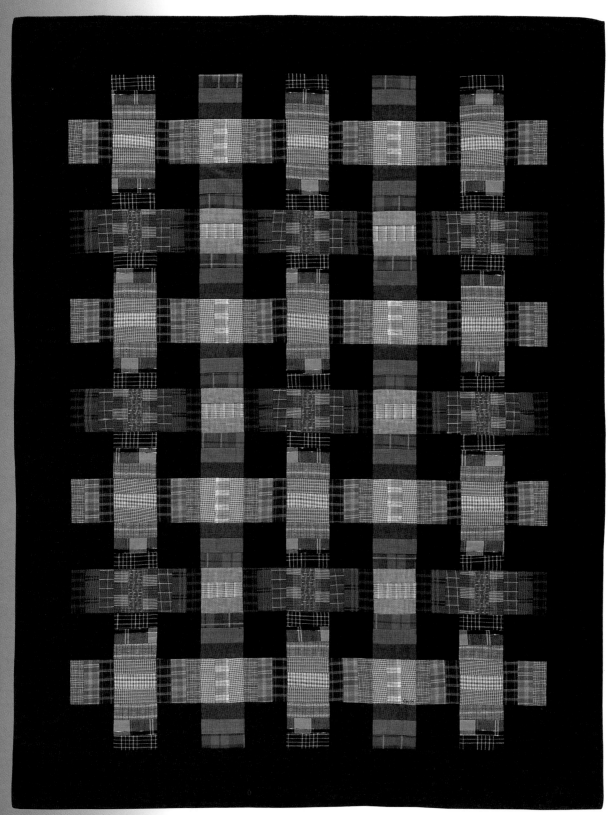

Bob and Weave, 52" x 40"

Examples of fabrics graded by value

BEFORE YOU START

Fabric selection is very important in making the illusion of weaving appear. Paying attention to *value*—the relative lightness or darkness of a fabric—is important.

You will need 5 different fabrics, graded from light to dark (light, medium-light, medium, medium-dark, and dark). There should be even steps between each value. The illusion works best if the dark fabric is very close to black.

Label your fabrics to help avoid confusion. Number each set of fabrics within a color family from 1 to 5, with 1 being the lightest value and 5 being the darkest. Cut a small scrap of each fabric and tape it to a piece of paper for reference.

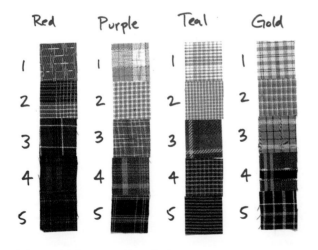

Label your fabrics to avoid confusion.

MATERIALS AND SUPPLIES

Woven bands of color (20 fabrics; fat quarters are fine):

- ¼ yard each of 5 values of red: light, medium-light, medium, medium-dark, dark
- ¼ yard each of 5 values of purple: light, medium-light, medium, medium-dark, dark
- ¼ yard each of 5 values of teal: light, medium-light, medium, medium-dark, dark
- ¼ yard each of 5 values of gold: light, medium-light, medium, medium-dark, dark

Background and border: 1¼ yards solid or near-solid dark fabric

Backing: 2½ yards

Batting: 44" x 56"

Binding: ½ yard

CUTTING

NOTE: *If you are using fat quarters for your color bands, double the number of strips you cut.*

HINT: You can stack the fabrics of each color family and cut four strips at once.

- Woven bands of color, values #2–5: Cut 2 strips 1½" x fabric width of each fabric (32 strips total).
- Woven bands of color, value #1: Cut 1 strip 1½" x fabric width of each fabric (4 strips total).
- Background: Cut 5 strips 3½" x fabric width; then cut the strips into 48 squares 3½" x 3½".
- Border: Cut 5 strips 4" x fabric width.

CONSTRUCTION

Strip Set Assembly

1. Sew the strips in sets of three as shown. You should have twice as many 3-4-5 sets as 2-1-2 sets. Press the seams toward the darker fabric.

Sew 2* strip sets of each color family.

3½"	3½"
3 (medium)	
4 (medium-dark)	

Red 3-4-5 (2 strip sets)

3½"	3½"
3 (medium)	
4 (medium-dark)	

Purple 3-4-5 (2 strip sets)*

3½"	3½"
3 (medium)	
4 (medium-dark)	
5 (dark)	

Teal 3-4-5 (2 strip sets)

3½"	3½"
3 (medium)	
4 (medium-dark)	
5 (dark)	

Gold 3-4-5 (2 strip sets)*

Sew 1* strip set of each color family.

3½"	3½"
2 (medium-light)	
1 (light)	
2 (medium-light)	

Red 2-1-2 (1 strip set)

3½"	3½"
2 (medium-light)	
1 (light)	
2 (medium-light)	

Purple 2-1-2 (1 strip set)

3½"	3½"
2 (medium-light)	
1 (light)	
2 (medium-light)	

Teal 2-1-2 (1 strip set)

3½"	3½"
2 (medium-light)	
1 (light)	
2 (medium-light)	

Gold 2-1-2 (1 strip set)*

*You may need to make 1 more strip set if your fabric is less than 42" wide. If you are using fat quarters, double the number of strip sets you make.

2. Cut the strip sets into squares, 3½" x 3½". You will need the following number of squares:

Red 2-1-2	9
Red 3-4-5	18
Purple 2-1-2	8
Purple 3-4-5	24
Teal 2-1-2	6
Teal 3-4-5	16
Gold 2-1-2	12
Gold 3-4-5	24
Background	48

Quilt Construction

1. Lay out the blocks on your design wall. Orienting the blocks correctly is important. Refer to the diagram.

2. Sew the blocks together into rows horizontally. Press the seams in each row in an alternate direction so the seams will nest together when the rows are sewn together.

3. Sew the rows together, matching seams. Press the seams in one direction.

4. Sew the 5 strips of border fabric together, end to end. Press the seams open. This will allow for long enough borders to go all around the quilt.

5. Measure the quilt through the center vertically to calculate the length of the side borders. Cut 2 border strips to this measurement and sew them to the sides of the quilt, easing if necessary. Press the seams toward the border.

6. Measure the quilt (plus side borders) through the center horizontally to calculate the length of the top and bottom borders. Cut 2 border strips to this measurement and sew them to top and bottom of the quilt, easing if necessary. Press the seams toward the border.

QUILTING AND FINISHING

1. Layer and baste the quilt top, batting, and backing.

2. Quilt by hand or machine using your preferred design, or quilt in the ditch.

3. Block the quilt. Lay out the quilt on a large horizontal surface such as the floor. Smooth the quilt into shape. Steam the quilt with a steam iron until damp. Allow the quilt to dry completely, (usually overnight), before picking it up.

4. Bind.

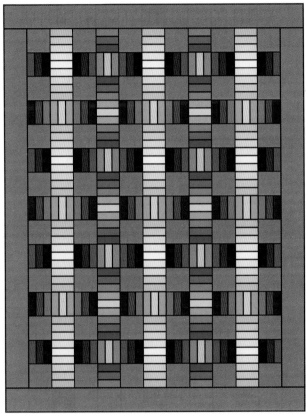

Quilt construction

Piecing is fun——it's my favorite way to quilt. I consider piecing one of my most important tools for creating a sense of depth.

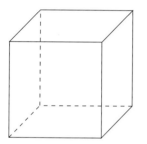

Adding perspective makes a square look like a three-dimensional cube.

I've learned to incorporate shadows into my pieced designs to create a three-dimensional look. With just a little planning (a little bit of drafting ability really helps), you can design shadows right into your pieced design—shadows that will visually lift your blocks right off the surface of your quilt.

I use both *perspective settings* and *drop shadows* when I design a pieced quilt. Let me describe what I mean by those terms.

PERSPECTIVE SETTINGS

Back in second grade, one of my artistic friends showed me how to draw a cube. All it took was the simple addition of a few lines of perspective to go from a flat square to a cube that looked three-dimensional. I thought that was the coolest thing! I still do—only now I apply it to quilt settings.

The perspective setting is easy and fun. When you set your quilt block with a perspective setting, the block appears to be on one face of a cube. This technique is most effective when you are setting blocks with sashing strips and a border of the same background fabric.

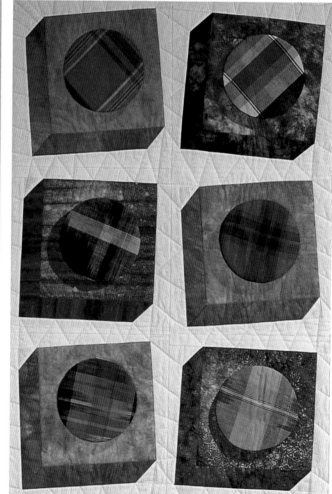

Stumbling Blocks detail
(full quilt page 107)

Adding Perspective Settings to Quilt Blocks

Imagine that your quilt block is on one face of a cube. When you look at that face of the cube from this angle, you can see slivers of two other faces of the cube. This is the effect we are aiming for.

What color should the other faces be? Well, they can be any color you like, but in my opinion, the most effective color is a darker, duller, grayer version of the background of the quilt block. Sound familiar? The difference between choosing a color for a shadow and choosing a color for a perspective setting is this: For a shadow, the shadow color is a darker, duller shade of the *sashing/border fabric*, whereas for a perspective setting, the color of the other faces is a darker, duller shade of the *quilt block fabric*.

In other words, the fabric in a perspective setting relates to the color of the block and not to the color of the sashing or background of the quilt itself. Each block may have a different fabric for its perspective setting, if you have used several colors in the block backgrounds.

You might also consider using two fabrics for the perspective setting: one fabric darker and duller than the block fabric, and the other even darker and duller than that. This gives the impression that one face of the cube is slightly better lit than the bottom.

Basic Perspective Setting Recipe

This basic recipe is vague and general. It's like the way your grandma cooked—a handful of this and a pinch of that, depending on her mood, her taste, and the ingredients at hand. You can modify this recipe so it works for your particular quilt. The width of the perspective strips depends on the size of your blocks; a rule of thumb is that the perspective strips should be no wider than one-third the width of the block. They can be as narrow as you like. But even that is up to you.

It's easy to audition this setting. Lay out a few blocks on your background fabric. Cut a few perspective strips and lay them along the bottom and side of each block, folding back the corners diagonally to create a cube. Audition a few different widths before you make a decision.

INGREDIENTS
- One or more quilt blocks (pieced, appliquéd, plain), any size, that
  you would like to put into a perspective setting
- Background fabric for sashing and border
- Fabric to create perspective (a darker, duller color than the block fabric)

The fabric color of a perspective setting relates to the color of the block.

Using two colors creates the effect of realistic lighting.

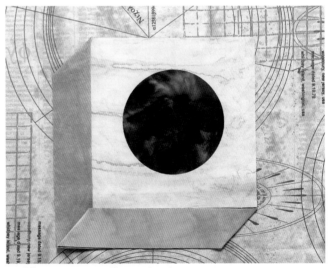

Audition your perspective setting.

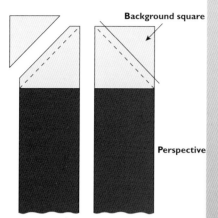

Background square

Perspective

Add background triangles to the ends of perspective strips. Trim away excess fabric.

1. Cut 2 strips from the *perspective* fabric. The width depends on the size of the block. About ¼ the width of the block is a nice proportion. Each strip should be as long as one side of the block, plus the width of the perspective strip.

2. From the *background* fabric, cut 2 squares the same size as the width of the perspective strip.

3. Sew one square of the background fabric diagonally across each end of the perspective fabric strip to form a triangle. Orientation is important! Trim away the excess background and perspective fabrics underneath to ¼". Press the seam toward the darker fabric.

4. Sew these strips to the bottom and left-hand edges of the quilt block with the background triangles placed as shown. Sew a mitered seam at the corner where the two perspective strips come together.

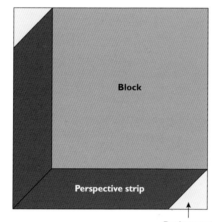

Block

Perspective strip

Background

Add strips to two sides of the block to form a "cube." Note the orientation of the background triangles.

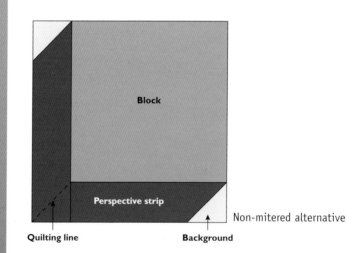

Block

Perspective strip

Quilting line

Background

Non-mitered alternative

The corner triangles disappear into the sashing and border fabric, leaving the impression of a three-dimensional cube.

5. Sash the blocks with the background fabric, any width you like.

6. Once set, the blocks can be oriented in any direction you prefer.

7. Add a border of the background fabric, any width you choose.

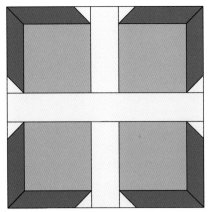
Cubes can be oriented in any direction.

DROP SHADOWS

Imagine a piece of paper floating above the surface of a table. A light from above the table is shining on the paper at an angle. As you look down at the paper, you see its shadow along two of its edges (which edges will depend on your position and the position of the light source). The shadow appears disconnected from the paper. It has the same shape as the paper but it is off on a diagonal a bit. This is a *drop shadow*.

The object that casts the shadow (the paper, in this case) is two-dimensional. It's flat. We can assume the background is two-dimensional also (the surface of a table). Flat again. It's adding the *shadow* that makes the scene appear three-dimensional because the shadow visually "floats" the object off the surface. We can do the same thing with our quilt blocks—float them right off the surface of the background—just by adding a shadow.

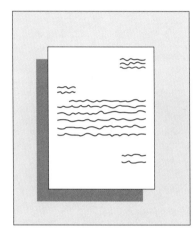
Adding a drop shadow makes the paper appear to float above the table.

Adding Drop Shadows to Quilt Blocks

The simplest way to describe adding a drop shadow to a quilt block is to make a few basic assumptions.

Family Monuments detail (full quilt page 102)

- All the quilt blocks are the same size.
- They are all floating at the same distance above the surface of the background.
- The light source is toward the upper right-hand corner of the quilt, and it's very far away, like the sun.

With these things in mind, we can create a drop shadow that requires no math or drafting skills whatsoever.

Basic Drop Shadow Recipe

This is a generic recipe for adding a drop shadow to a block-based quilt. The recipe can be expanded or adapted to fit anything you might want to "float," as long as you understand why the technique works in the first place.

First of all, you have to create the idea of a background. By using sashing and a border of the same fabric, it appears as if you have laid your blocks down on a flat surface, like a table. Just open a yard or two of background fabric and audition your blocks by laying them out in an orderly fashion on this background: You have now created the appearance of a background. All you have to do is "lift" those blocks and let them cast a shadow on this background. You can do this visually by adding that shadow along two sides of each block.

Since the little corners of the shadow strips are the same fabric as the sashing and border, they disappear, leaving only the shadows noticeable. The blocks appear to float!

INGREDIENTS
- One or more quilt blocks (pieced, appliquéd, plain), any size, that you would like to "float"
- Background fabric for sashing and border (anything except black)
- Shadow fabric to create pieced shadows (See Chapter 1 for color discussion; briefly, shadow fabric should be a darker, duller, grayer color than the background fabric.)

1. Cut 2 strips from the *shadow* fabric, a little longer than the side or bottom of each block.

2. Cut 2 squares the same size as the width of the shadow strips from the *background* fabric for each block.

3. Sew one square of background fabric to the end of each shadow fabric strip. Press toward the darker fabric.

4. Sew these strips "log-cabin style" to the bottom and left-hand edges of the quilt block with the background squares along the outside corners.

5. Sash the blocks with the background fabric, any width you like.

6. Add a border of the background fabric, any width you choose.

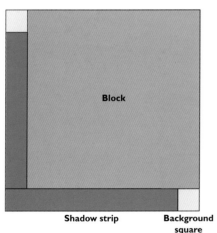

Shadow strip   **Background square**

Add background squares to the ends of the shadow strips.

Block

Shadow strip   **Background square**

Add shadow strips to the blocks. Note the placement of the background squares.

Alternatives

Like any good recipe, this basic recipe can be tweaked any way you like. Check out the following ideas from our discussion of shadows in Chapter 1 —they are all easy to apply to piecing.

- Move the light source from the right to the left.
- Allow the light to rise or set.
- Move the light source (or your quilt) to a different angle.
- Float your blocks at different heights.
- Bring the light closer—make it a desk lamp instead of the sun.

Alder, 41" x 33".
The blocks appear to float at different heights above the background.

Floating an Alternate Block Setting

Suppose you prefer a different setting than the traditional sashing. Maybe you would rather alternate your pieced or appliquéd blocks with plain background blocks. You can still "float" your blocks by adding shadows to the alternate background blocks.

Imagine that your quilt blocks are connected just by the tips of their corners and have been lifted off the surface of the background. They would form a grid that would cast shadows you would see in the squares between them—on the plain background blocks. If we add those shadows along two sides of the background blocks, we can create the illusion that the pieced or appliquéd blocks are floating.

An alternate setting creates some interesting shadow problems when you come to the edge. They are fairly easy to fix depending on your choice of border treatments.

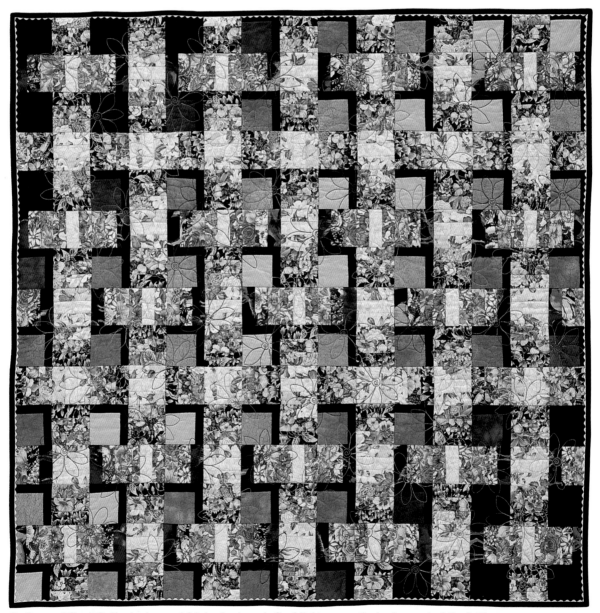

Radiance, *47" x 47". The background fabrics imply a shaft of light across the background of the lattice. There is no border on this quilt—the blocks go all the way to the edge.*

Floating Nine-Patch,
29" x 29". A border of a
different fabric encroaches
into the alternate blocks.

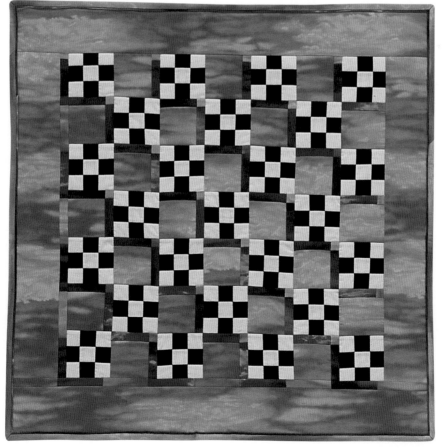

Floating Nine-Patch 2,
29" x 29". The border is
the same fabric as the
alternate blocks, so the
shadows extend into the
border on two sides.

Adding Drop Shadows to Elements Within Blocks

So far we have floated entire blocks off the surface of the quilt, but we can also float elements *within* a quilt block.

Cluster Class detail (full quilt page 99)

For example, we can float Nine-Patch blocks, or we can float the elements of the Nine-Patch block.

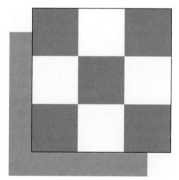

Floating an entire Nine-Patch block

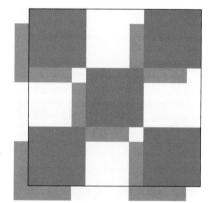

Floating patches within the Nine-Patch block

The principles for floating elements within a block are the same as for floating the blocks themselves.

Piecing is a versatile way to float all kinds of objects in a quilt. Perspective and drop shadows are concepts that can be stretched and applied in so many ways. You might become a graph paper doodler!

Emerald City

Granite headstones in a peaceful cemetery inspired this quilt. I love walking in cemeteries. I wanted to capture the feeling of fleeting shadows and eternal permanence, and the colors and carving of the granite.

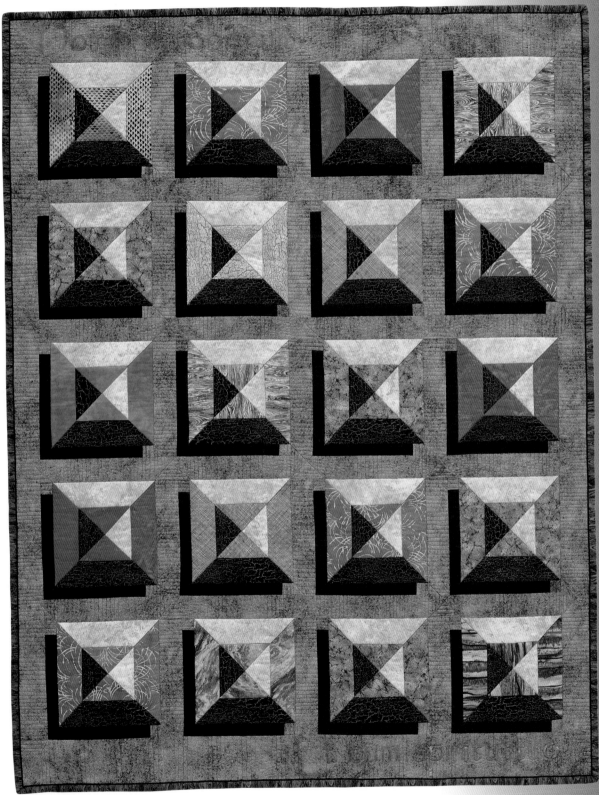

Emerald City, 50¾" x 40½"

BEFORE YOU START

Be sure to pay attention to *value* when choosing your fabrics. You will need three fabrics with different values for your blocks: dark, medium, and light.

You will also need a sashing/border fabric for the background and another fabric for its shadow. The shadow fabric should be a darker, duller, grayer shade of the sashing/border fabric, regardless of the block fabrics. If you aren't sure about a shadow fabric, try gray or black. It should be significantly darker than the sashing fabric, but not extremely so.

MATERIALS AND SUPPLIES

Blocks (fat quarters are fine):
- ½ yard dark-value fabric
- ½ yard light-value fabric
- 1 yard total of assorted medium-value fabrics (strips should measure at least 16" long—fat quarters are great)

Shadows: ½ yard of fabric that is darker and duller than the sashing/border fabric. If in doubt, use charcoal gray or black.

Sashing/borders: 1¼ yards solid or near-solid fabric

Backing: 2½ yards

Batting: 44" x 55"

Binding: ½ yard

Triangle ruler: Omnigrid #98 or 98L, for quarter-square triangles

CUTTING

NOTE: *If you are using fat quarters for your blocks, double the number of strips that you cut.*

Blocks:
- Dark fabric: Cut 5 strips 2¼" x fabric width.
- Light fabric: Cut 5 strips 2¼" x fabric width.
- Medium fabric: Cut 10 strips 2¼" x fabric width. If you are using more than one color of medium-value fabric, cut an even number of strips (at least 2) of each color.

Shadow strip sets:
- Sashing fabric: Cut 2 strips 1¼" x fabric width.
- Shadow fabric: Cut 1 strip 6¾" x fabric width. Cut 1 strip 7½" x fabric width.

Sashing: Cut 8 strips 2" x fabric width.

Borders: Cut 2 strips 3½" x fabric width for top and bottom borders. Cut 3 strips 2½" x fabric width for side borders.

CONSTRUCTION

Block Assembly

1. Sew the light and medium strips together. Press the seams toward the medium fabric.

2. Sew the dark and medium strips together. Press the seams toward the medium fabric.

NOTE: *If you have used more than one color of medium-value fabric, you should have an even number of strips (at least 2) of each medium color. For each color, sew one medium strip to a dark strip and the other medium strip to a light strip.*

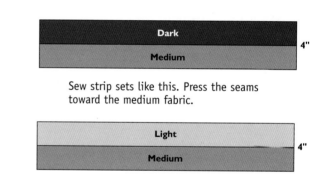

Sew strip sets like this. Press the seams toward the medium fabric.

3. Cut triangles from the strip sets using the triangle ruler. Flip the ruler to cut triangles from the opposite side of the strip. You will get two kinds of triangles from each strip set—those with the medium fabric at the base and those with the medium fabric at the tip.

WISE TIP To line up the triangle, use the center seam, not the edge of the strip. Strip edges can be wavy or warped, and they won't show anyway.

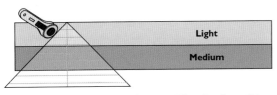

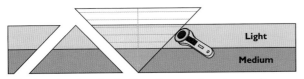

Cut triangles from the strip sets. Triangles from this side have medium fabric at the base.

Flip the triangle ruler to the other side to cut opposite triangles. These triangles have medium fabric at the tip.

You will need 20 of each of the following triangles:

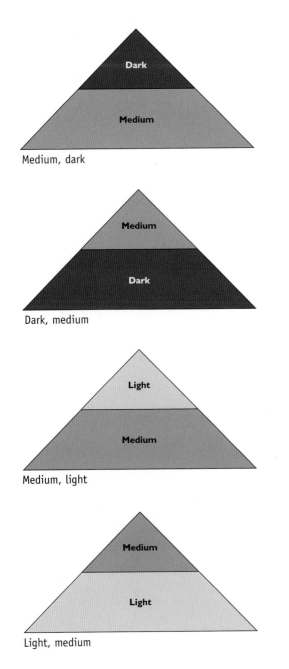

Medium, dark

Dark, medium

Medium, light

Light, medium

4. Sew the triangles together. The orientation of the triangles is important to maintain a consistent light source. Press the seams toward the triangle with the medium base. Press the center seam to one side. The block will measure 7½" x 7½".

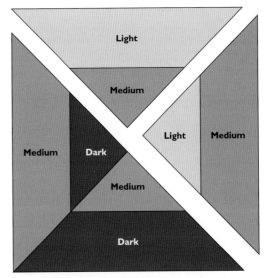

Block construction

Adding Shadow Strips

1. Sew a narrow (1¼") sashing strip to each of the wider shadow strips. These are shadow strip sets. Press the seams in either direction.

2. Cut 20 slices, 1¼" wide, from each shadow strip set.

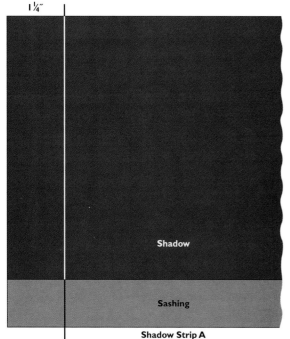

Cut 1¼" slices from each shadow strip set

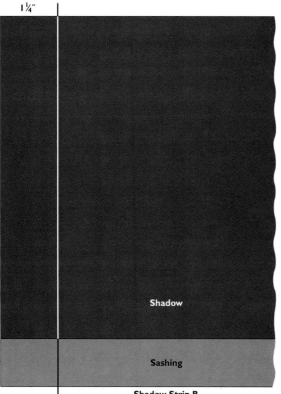

3. Sew slices from shadow strip set A along the bottom of the block as shown. Sew slices from shadow strip set B along the left edge of the block. Be sure that your block is in the proper orientation before sewing the shadows. The top of the block is the triangle with the light base; the bottom of the block is the triangle with the dark base. Press the seams toward the shadows.

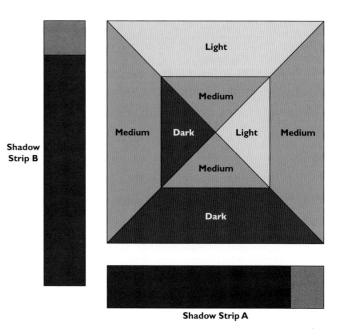

Sew the shadows to the block.

QUILT CONSTRUCTION

1. Lay out the blocks on your design wall. Be sure your shadowed blocks are oriented properly.

2. Sew the blocks to the 2" sashing strips; then trim the sashing and sew the blocks into rows horizontally. Press the seams toward the sashing.

3. Sew the rows together with 2" sashing strips. Press the seams toward the sashing.

4. Sew the 3 strips of 2½" border fabric together, end to end. Press the seams open. This will allow for long enough borders for both sides of the quilt.

5. Measure the quilt through the center vertically to calculate the length of the side borders. Cut 2 border strips to this measurement and sew them to the sides of the quilt, easing if necessary. Press the seams toward the border.

6. Measure the quilt (plus side borders) through the center horizontally to calculate the length of the top and bottom borders. Cut both 3½" border strips to this measurement and sew them to the top and bottom of the quilt, easing if necessary. Press the seams toward the border.

QUILTING AND FINISHING

1. Layer and baste the quilt top, batting, and backing.

2. Quilt by hand or machine using your preferred design, or quilt in the ditch.

3. Block the quilt. Lay out the quilt on a large horizontal surface such as the floor. Smooth the quilt into shape. Steam the quilt with a steam iron until damp. Allow the quilt to dry completely, (usually overnight), before picking it up.

4. Bind.

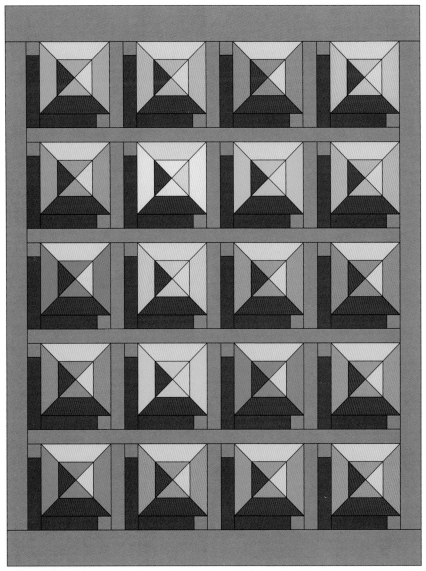

Quilt construction

Chapter Four

APPLIQUÉD SHADOWS

The concepts of using shadows also apply to appliqué, whether by hand, machine, or fusible web. By adding shadows to appliqué, we can create a greater sense of depth and dimension.

APPLIQUÉD DROP SHADOWS

One method of creating a sense of depth is to appliqué a *drop shadow* behind each individual appliqué piece that you would like to "float." The shadow creates the illusion that that particular piece is hovering above the surface of its surroundings.

A drop shadow is simply the shadow that an object would cast if that object were floating an inch or two above the surface. You see drop shadows everywhere—lettering on signs and buildings, some of the "buttons" on your computer screen. We've looked at using drop shadows in piecing in Chapter 3. We can use drop shadows in appliqué too.

A drop shadow is easy to create for appliqué. The shadow will be the same size and shape as the object that is casting the shadow. It will just be offset a little when applied to the background.

Picture a circle appliquéd onto a background, as in the illustration below. It's just a flat circle on a flat surface, a plate on a table.

If we add a drop shadow behind the circle, it seems to float off the surface a little bit. Have you ever seen a collectible plate or a piece of art glass on display on a wall? The plate seems to hover just above the surface. It casts a shadow on the wall behind it. We're recreating that look here. It's more three-dimensional.

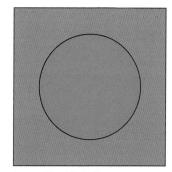
An appliquéd circle appears to be flat.

An appliquéd circle with a drop shadow appears to be floating.

This works well if the appliqué piece to be shadowed is relatively large and simple—so you wouldn't want to add a shadow for every flower petal in a bouquet. It also helps if the shadowed pieces are not overlapping each other—conflicting shadows are more complicated to work out, for both the quilter and the viewer.

You can see the effect of a drop shadow in *Eclipse*. Each of the smaller "satellite" circles has its own drop shadow appliquéd behind it. The shadows make the satellites look as if they are circling the larger "planets" and casting a shadow down on them.

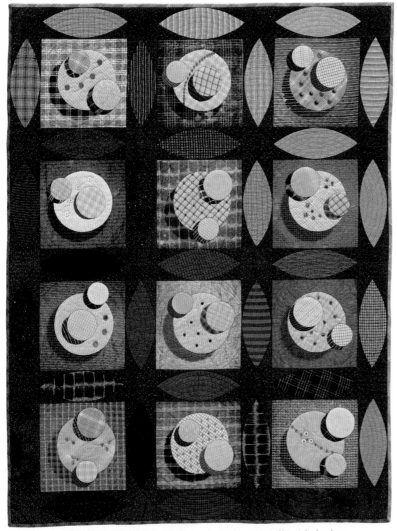

Eclipse, 51" x 40". Techniques: discharged shadows, appliquéd shadows.

Eclipse detail. Note that the smaller circles have appliquéd shadows

It's simple to create an appliqué drop shadow. Just cut an extra shape, the same size and shape as the piece you want to shadow, but cut it out of *shadow fabric*. A shadow fabric, remember, is just a darker, duller, grayer version of the *background fabric*. Suppose you want to float a circle on your quilt. It doesn't matter if the circle is a neon bright novelty print or a muted Civil War reproduction fabric—the shadow relates to the background, not to the piece itself. All the shadows on a given background should be the same color.

There are two ways you can add an appliqué drop shadow:

- Appliqué the shadows directly to the background, either before adding the appliqué pieces, or at the same time. Mark out your pattern, and baste or pin the shadows in place.

Sew or fuse shadows directly to the background before adding appliqué pieces.

Add shadows to appliqué pieces to create units, which can then be appliquéd to the background.

■ Or appliqué the shadow directly to the piece that it will be shadowing, and then add that unit to the background as one piece.

When I use the second method, I always feel like Wendy sewing Peter Pan's shadow to his toes. In *Eclipse* (page 45), I appliquéd the darker shadow circles to each satellite circle first. Once I had them done, I positioned the units, satellite plus shadow, the way I liked and appliquéd them to the background.

If you are fusing, you can create these units using an appliqué pressing sheet, which allows you to press fusibles together without sticking them to a background fabric. Here's how:

1. Iron fusible web to the backs of all your fabrics.

2. Trace and cut out your shapes, including shadows, and peel off the backing paper.

3. Iron your fused piece to its shadow, with both pieces fusible side down, on the nonstick appliqué pressing sheet.

4. Allow the unit to cool and peel it off in one piece.

5. Fuse the unit to the background.

Using an appliqué pressing sheet, fuse your pieces to the shadows before adding them to the background.

Direction Is Important!

Whichever method you use to add shadows, it's important to make sure that your shadows fall in a consistent direction. Consider where your implied light source is located. If your light source is in the upper right corner of your quilt, all the shadows should fall away from the light—that is, below and to the left of the objects that are casting the shadows. Shadows always fall in the opposite direction of the light source. It doesn't make sense if some of the shadows fall to the left and some to the right. Be logical and consistent when placing your shadows.

Just about everything we learned about piecing drop shadows (pages 33–35) applies to appliquéing drop shadows as well. You can change the direction, distance, and angle of the light source, float your pieces at different heights, or add drop shadows to elements within the blocks.

Too Many "Shadows," Not Enough Words

Here's where there is no good vocabulary to describe what I want to say. I end up using the word "shadow" too many times! Here it is in a nutshell: *Don't let your shadow piece "shadow through" your floating piece.*

What I'm trying to get across is that even though you are adding a shadow to an appliqué piece, you don't want to see that darker shadow through the surface of that piece. You want to see the shadow only *outside* of the actual piece. Those of you who do appliqué probably already know that when you appliqué a lighter fabric on top of a darker fabric, the darker fabric may "shadow through." You can cut away the excess darker fabric under the lighter piece to prevent this. If you are fusing, it's even more important to cut away any part of the shadow that shadows through the piece; because the pieces are literally stuck together, it's much easier to see the shadow through the piece.

SHEER SHADOWS

Most quilters head straight for the cottons when they enter a fabric store. We hurry past all those fashion fabrics on our way to the "good stuff." Let's not be so hasty. Back up a minute, and let's have a look at those sheers.

Shadows are actually sheer, when you think about it. They don't stain the ground or leave any lasting mark. They aren't so dense and impenetrable that you can't see through them; you can wave your hand through someone else's shadow and still see your hand. All shadows do is temporarily darken the area they cover.

So consider using sheer fabrics for shadows. There are several advantages to using sheers:

- If you are confused about what color to make your appliquéd or fused shadows, you can pretty much always use a gray, brown, or black sheer.
- If the background you are using is mottled, the shadow color you need may not be consistent. And if the background is a print, you might not be able to find the right "darker, duller" companion print that makes a convincing shadow.
- If your background is pieced and the shadow falls across several different fabrics, using a sheer for your shadows can darken all the background fabrics equally.

There are also disadvantages to using sheers:

- Hand and machine appliqué do not work with sheers, because you can see the turned-under seam allowance. Real shadows don't have seam allowances.
- Raw-edge appliqué can also be difficult, because sheers can be difficult to work with in their raw (unstabilized) state. They can be stretchy and bias-y, and some of them fray unmercifully. And stabilizing them with fusible interfacing destroys their sheerness.

Don't let your shadow pieces "shadow through"! Cut away excess shadow fabric behind your appliqué pieces.

Sheer fabrics can make great shadows.

You can use paper-backed fusible web to tame sheers. The web stabilizes the fabric—no more fraying and a lot less stretching—and makes it a lot easier to work with. And you can press it directly to your background.

The important thing to know when ironing fusible web to sheers is that the hot glue oozes right through the fabric. Ugh! This can really gum up an iron. And if you iron it upside down, it will stick your sheer right to your ironing board.

To avoid this, use an appliqué pressing sheet. If you don't have one, the leftover paper backing from the fusible web (that's the paper you peel off after fusing the web to the fabric) works well too. The glue on the fusible web does not adhere to either of these materials, so you can protect your iron and your ironing board. Just be sure that you are never ironing directly onto the sheer … and it never hurts to have some iron cleaner on hand, just in case.

Place an appliqué pressing sheet *under the sheer* to protect your ironing board when fusing the fusible web to the sheer. The paper on the fusible web will protect your iron.

Place the appliqué pressing sheet *on top of the sheer* when fusing the sheer shape to the background, to protect your iron.

Add your appliqué pieces after placing the shadows. Be aware that the fusible web makes the sheer rather stiff and hard to needle though, if you are appliquéing by hand. If you are fusing, you can place the entire composition together before pressing it onto the background.

As always, watch the orientation of the shadows—remember where your light source is and which direction the shadows should fall.

PUDDLED SHADOWS

Shadows don't always fall neatly behind an object. And sometimes they aren't shaped much like the object either. A leaf floating in a pond casts a shadow that looks like a leaf, but a tree in a yard can cast a shadow that doesn't look much like a tree. It looks more like a puddle at the base of the tree. But the shadow tells us that the tree is bulky; it has three dimensions. I call these "puddled shadows."

Puddled shadows have the advantage of being irregular. They relate to the object that creates the shadow, but they don't really look much like them. The great thing about that (for me) is they are easy to draw!

I'm used to viewing the world from a certain angle, which has to do with my height. You are, too. If I were to look at an object on a table, let's say a basket of flowers, I would be looking slightly down on it. I would see its shadow on the table, and I would see that the basket rests in the middle of its shadow. Its shadow is a flattened irregular shape.

If I were appliquéing a basket of flowers, I could add a puddled shadow to make my basket a little more three-dimensional. The basket will sit right in the middle of its shadow. If the basket is placed above its shadow, it will look as if it is hovering in mid-air, which might be okay for a ball or a leaf but is pretty unusual for a basket. Use a reducing lens, or step back from your composition, to make sure that your placement is convincing.

Puddled shadows can be created with shadow fabric (a darker, duller version of the background fabric) or with a fused sheer fabric. Add the puddled shadow to the background before adding the other appliqué pieces. It's a simple way to add extra interest to your appliqué.

The basket rests in the middle of its shadow.

The appliquéd basket also rests in the middle of its shadow.

Wild Sky

Planets and satellites wheel and dance through a daytime sky. It's not often that we see an eclipse during the day. What's going on?

Wild Sky, 58" x 42½"

BEFORE YOU START

To create a three-dimensional look to the blocks, choose a perspective fabric that is a darker, duller shade of the fabric used as the background of the blocks.

MATERIALS AND SUPPLIES

Blocks: 1 yard

Large circles: Scraps of assorted bright colors, ½ yard total

Small and medium circle shadows: ¼ yard of fabric that is darker and duller than the circle fabrics

Perspective fabric and large circle shadows: 1 yard

Sashing and border: 1½ yards

Backing: 2⅝ yards

Batting: 62" x 47"

Binding: ½ yard

CUTTING

Blocks:
- Cut 3 strips 9½" x fabric width; then cut the strips into 12 squares, 9½" x 9½".

Circles:
- Cut 12 large circles, 6½" in diameter, using the cutting line on the template pattern on page 55, from bright fabrics.
- Cut 12 medium circles, 3½" in diameter, using the cutting line on the template pattern on page 55, from bright fabrics.
- Cut 12 small circles, 2½" in diameter, using the cutting line on the template pattern on page 55, from bright fabrics.

Circle shadows:
- Cut 12 large circles, 6½" in diameter, from perspective fabric.
- Cut 12 medium circles, 3½" in diameter, from shadow fabric.
- Cut 12 small circles, 2½" in diameter, from shadow fabric.

WISE TIP The shadow fabric for the large circles will be the same as the perspective fabric. The smaller circles may have a different shadow fabric, which should relate to the fabric in the large circles.

Perspective setting:
- Cut 8 strips 2" x fabric width; then cut 24 pieces 11½" long. Trim a 45° angle from one end for a miter. Trim 12 pieces in one direction and 12 in the other.

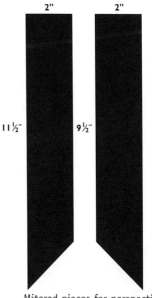

Mitered pieces for perspective setting, 12 pieces each

Sashing squares:
- Cut 2 strips 2" x fabric width; then cut the strips into 24 squares, 2" x 2".

Sashing:
- Cut 6 strips 2½" x fabric width.

Border:
- Cut 3 strips 4" x fabric width for side borders.
- Cut 3 strips 5½" x fabric width for top and bottom borders.

CONSTRUCTION

Circles are a challenge because it's so obvious when they are not quite right. It's much easier if a machine would stamp out a perfect circle for you. Try this method for appliquéing circles by hand or machine.

First, you need a pressing template—a heat-proof circle of the finished size. It's not a coincidence that the large circles in this quilt are the size of those inexpensive paper plates (dessert size)—they make great pressing templates! Just flatten one with an iron and you have a perfect 6"-diameter circle. The smaller circles are the size of very thin washers I found in a local hardware store. Baste the edge of the fabric circle by hand or machine. Place the pressing template in the middle of the fabric circle and pull the ends of the basting thread to gather the edges. Distribute the gathers evenly around the edges of the circle—no puckers! Press the circle, template and all. Use spray sizing to get a nice crisp edge. Remove the template and press again. You will have a nice crisp circle with the seam allowance already pressed under, ready to appliqué by hand or machine.

Gather the edge of the circle around the paper plate and press.

Block Assembly

1. Appliqué the large circle shadow to each block. See page 47 if your shadow fabric shows through your large-circle fabric.

2. Appliqué the large bright circle to each block, leaving 1" of the shadow circle showing in the lower left.

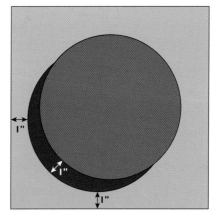

Placement for the large circle and its shadow

3. Appliqué the medium and small circle shadows to the blocks, on top of the large circles. Experiment with the placement; make each one a little different!

4. Appliqué the medium and small bright circles to their shadows. For the medium circle, leave ⅝" of the shadow circle showing in the lower left. For the small circle, leave ½" of the shadow circle showing.

Perspective Setting

1. Sew a "sew and flip" triangle at the square end of each mitered piece (pages 32–33). Place a 2" sashing square on the square end of a mitered perspective piece. With right sides together, sew the corner diagonally. The angle of the seam will be the same as the angle of the miter cut.

Sew sashing corners to mitered perspective pieces.

2. Press the seam toward the corner. Trim the seam allowance under the triangle to ¼".

3. Make sure your block is oriented correctly; the circle shadows should be toward the lower left corner. Sew a perspective piece to the left side of each block. Stop and backstitch ¼" from the edge of the cut miter. Press the seam toward the perspective piece.

4. Sew a perspective piece to the bottom of each block. Stop and backstitch ¼" from the edge of the cut miter. Press the seam toward the perspective piece.

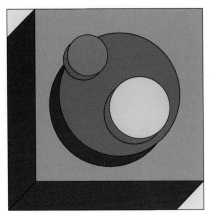

Sew perspective pieces to each block.

5. Sew the diagonal seam along the miter, backstitching at the inside corner. Press the seam to one side.

QUILT CONSTRUCTION

1. Lay out the blocks on your design wall. Be sure your perspective blocks are oriented properly.

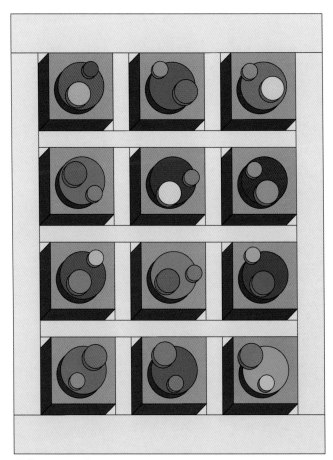

Quilt construction

2. Sew the blocks to the 2½" sashing strips; then trim the sashing and sew the blocks into rows horizontally. Press the seams toward the sashing.

3. Sew the rows together with 2½" sashing strips. Press the seams toward the sashing.

4. Sew the 3 strips of 4" border fabric together, end to end. Press the seams open. This will allow for long enough borders for both sides of the quilt.

5. Measure the quilt through the center vertically to calculate the length of the side borders. Cut 2 border strips to this measurement and sew them to the sides of the quilt, easing if necessary. Press the seams toward the border.

6. Sew 3 strips of 5½" border fabric together, end to end. Press the seams open. This will allow for long enough borders for both side of the quilt.

7. Measure the quilt (plus side borders) through the center horizontally to calculate the length of the top and bottom borders. Cut 2 border strips to this measurement and sew them to the top and bottom of the quilt, easing if necessary. Press the seams toward the border.

QUILTING AND FINISHING

1. Layer and baste the quilt top, batting, and backing.

2. Quilt by hand or machine using your preferred design, or quilt in the ditch.

3. Block the quilt. Lay out the quilt on a large horizontal surface such as the floor. Smooth the quilt into shape. Steam the quilt with a steam iron until damp. Allow the quilt to dry completely, (usually overnight), before picking it up.

4. Bind.

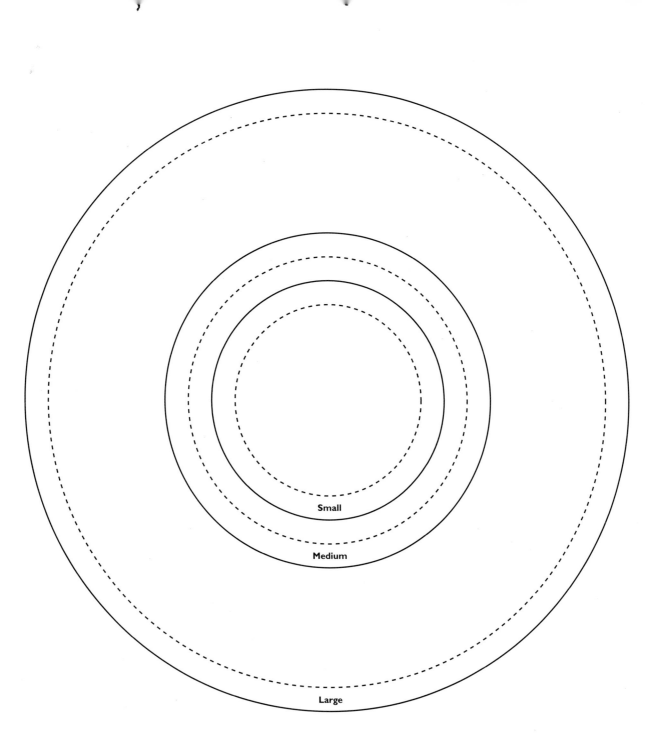

Small

Medium

Large

6 CIRCLE PATTERNS
Use outer circle of each size for cutting and inner circle for pressing.

Chapter Five

If you look at a shadow on a sunny day, you'll notice that no matter how bright the sun is, the edges of the shadow are not sharp, distinct lines. A little light bends around the object, which blurs the edge of the shadow. Discharging (removing) the dye from your fabric is a great way to recreate those realistic blurry shadows. I love using this technique to create quilts that look three-dimensional. And the best part is that you can easily do it with common household chemicals!

WHAT IS DISCHARGING?

Discharging is the process of removing dye from fabric. Maybe you've done it before. I know I have; I've accidentally discharged many a sweater sleeve in my laundry room while adding bleach to a load of whites.

There are a number of processes that remove or change the dye in fabric. The simplest process involves light itself, which tends to fade fabric. The problem with light for our purposes is that it just takes too long. We are looking for instant gratification, a process that will work quickly, safely, and effectively. Let's look instead at a powerful common household chemical— chlorine bleach.

But first, this important announcement.
BLEACH IS DANGEROUS!

I like using bleach to discharge fabrics. It's cheap, easily available, effective, and quick—but it is definitely not safe. Please read the Safety Precautions (page 60) carefully before using bleach as a discharge agent!

SELECTING YOUR DESIGN

Choosing your design is the most fun part. Any shape goes! Your only limitation is your ability to cut out or appliqué the design— simple leaves like oaks are easy to cut out; lacy compound leaves like ferns are a challenge.

Templates and Masks

Let's clarify the distinction between a *mask* and a *template*, as I use the terms here:

- A *template* is a shape that will be traced to make an appliquéd or fused piece. The template is the shape that appears to cast the shadow on the background fabric.
- A *mask* is a covering used in discharging that prevents the bleach solution from reaching the fabric underneath it. The area under the mask will remain the original color of the fabric. The mask leaves the shadow on the background fabric.

Templates and masks can be the very same thing, serving both purposes. A shape can serve first as a template, for copying the shape so that you can apply it to the background, and second as a mask to create the shadow of the shape on the background fabric as you discharge it. Once something— paper, leaves, or whatever—has been used as a mask, it will be soaked with bleach. Unless you are using plastic, metal, or something else that can be washed thoroughly, you can just throw the mask away when you're finished with it. Be sure to discard any bleach-soaked masks directly into a garbage can with a tightly fitting lid, or allow them to air-dry outside before discarding them.

Real-life example: I like to use leaves in my work. First, I use the leaves as templates, tracing around them on fusible web (or freezer paper, for hand or machine appliqué). Then I lay them on the background fabric and use them as masks while I discharge. After they have been used as masks, I throw them out.

Obviously, I like to use leaves. What else can be used for masks and templates? The choices are unlimited! Anything flat will work—and that includes anything you can cut out of paper. Can't you just think of a million things?

Using Paper for Templates and Masks

Using paper for templates and masks creates unlimited possibilities. Anything you can cut out of paper can be used as a mask. Imagine printing large lettering on your computer, cutting it out, and using the letters as masks to create floating text! How about tracing the profiles of your children (or grandchildren) on paper and creating floating silhouettes? Circles, stars, hearts—really, any geometric shape can be cut out of paper. And what could be easier than abstract shapes? (Of course, it goes without saying that you should be sensitive to copyright issues.)

The type of paper you use as a mask makes a difference in the discharging process. If the paper is too absorbent, bleach can bleed through the paper onto the fabric below, defeating the purpose of the mask. If the paper is too waxy, the bleach beads up and the masks can be hard to pick up without spilling those bleach drops elsewhere on the fabric. Some papers curl when wetted, which can allow bleach to create a shape that is too indistinct to make a good shadow. Some become so floppy when wet that they can be hard to pick up.

The ideal paper is inexpensive, easily available, easy to cut, somewhat absorbent, and stays flat when wet. Bonus points if it can be run through a printer!

Here are the most useful papers, starting with the most effective:

- Card stock (sometimes called "index stock") is stiff enough to stay flat, thick enough to keep the bleach from seeping through, and absorbent enough to prevent the bleach from puddling up on top. It's easy to pick up off the fabric after spraying. It can be run through most computer printers, and it's inexpensive and easily available.
- Copy paper is almost as good as card stock.
- Watercolor paper too is almost as good as card stock, but it's more expensive and can't be run through a printer.
- Wonder Under fusible web backing paper is not as absorbent as the others but can be used successfully on dry fabric.

I don't recommend these papers:

- Freezer paper is difficult to remove, and leaks too much.
- Paper towels also leak too much, and they're too floppy to pick up.
- Construction paper is too soft and floppy, it's hard to pick up, and it leaks too much.

Using Leaves for Templates and Masks

If you are using leaves as your templates, try to find fresh green leaves. Although bright fall leaves are pretty, they are also brittle and frustrating to work with. Leaves are great because they come in such beautiful and varied shapes, they're cheap and easy to find, and they're completely disposable! Press them for a day or two to help them lie flat. Placing them between sheets of porous paper allows them to "breathe" as they flatten. For smaller leaves, a phone book is perfect. (At our house, we can't look up a phone number without a cascade of leaves falling out of the book. You might want to save an old phone book for this purpose.) If the leaves are larger, press them between sheets of newspaper and pile some books on top.

A note about fusible web products

I love using fusible web! It's fast and fun, and I can cut out those very sharp details that elude me when hand or machine appliquéing.

There are several paper-backed fusible web products on the market. Some of the brand names include Wonder Under, Heat-N-Bond, and Steam-A-Seam. Consider the following criteria in choosing a fusible web for this technique:

• The paper should stay on while you cut out your shapes. You will be drawing your design directly onto the paper backing and cutting out along those guidelines. If the paper is loose or falls off while you are cutting, it will totally drive you crazy!

• The fusible web should work well. The fused pieces should stick to the background. You should be able to iron the fused pieces over and over without loosening them. You should be able to handle your fused quilt without having the pieces fray excessively or, worse, actually fall off the quilt!

• The fused pieces should have a fairly supple hand. Fusing always involves a certain amount of stiffening of the fabric, but the amount varies from product to product. Hand quilting through fused fabric is always a challenge, but fusible that is too stiff can be difficult to quilt through even by machine.

Personally, my favorite currently available fusible web is Wonder Under. The paper stays on well, the hand is reasonably supple, it's acceptably archival, and I've had very few problems with the pieces releasing or fraying.

Appliqué Templates

You will be using your original shapes (for example, leaves or paper cutouts) in the template process. You'll also be using them as masks for discharging. After you've used them for discharging, they will be covered in bleach and fit only for the wastebasket. So use them as appliqué templates first.

It's important to pay attention to the orientation of the template. If the orientation of the appliqué piece is reversed, the discharged image will be the mirror image of the appliqué, which is not what you want.

If your piece is perfectly symmetrical (such as a circle) or has at least one line of symmetry (such as a heart), the orientation of the template will not matter. You can trace the template right side up or right side down. How can you tell if something is symmetrical? If you can draw a straight line somewhere through the middle of the shape so that both sides look exactly the same (through the middle of a heart, for example), your design is symmetrical.

But what if the object isn't symmetrical? Let's take those oak leaves, for example. We'll use the actual leaves as our masks for discharging in our project. They are not perfectly symmetrical; they are a little different on each side of the midrib. Therefore we will need to watch the orientation of the leaves as we work.

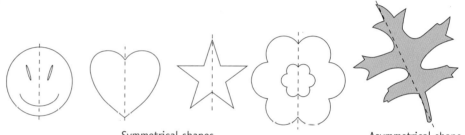

Symmetrical shapes   Asymmetrical shape

If you are planning to *fuse* the leaves to the surface, trace around each leaf on the paper side of your fusible web. Remember that the image is reversed (you are basically looking at the wrong side of your fabric when you look at the paper side of the fusible web), so place your leaves on the paper *right side down* when you trace. You will only use each leaf once. We'll trace them *right side down* for our templates, and use them *right side up* as our masks.

Using leaves for templates

Iron the fusible web to your chosen fabrics, following the manufacturer's instructions. Cut out the shapes. Remove the paper backing.

If you plan to *hand or machine appliqué* those leaves, trace the leaves onto freezer paper or directly onto fabric, as per your favorite appliqué technique. Be aware of the orientation of the leaf; you want the discharged image to be the same as the appliqué piece on top of it, and not its mirror image.

SELECTING BACKGROUND FABRIC

It is important that the fabric you select to discharge actually does *release dye (discharge)* when sprayed with a bleach solution. Your best bets are solid cottons, hand-dyed fabrics, and woven plaids. Basically, anything that looks the same on the front and back is a good candidate for discharging. Prints are made using inks, which are different from dyes and do not discharge as easily. Polyesters do not discharge.

Be sure to prewash your fabrics to remove any chemicals that may interfere with the discharging solution.

Fabrics will discharge differently depending on the dyes used. Two different black fabrics may look the same to your eye, but one may discharge to an earthy brown and the other to a flaming red. Be sure you have enough of the fabric and dye lot you want before you begin.

This may seem obvious, but you should like both the original color *and* the discharged color of the fabric. You might be surprised at some of the very ugly colors that you can get with discharging!

No matter which fabric you choose, be sure to test a small sample before you begin your project. I keep a small amount of 50:50 bleach solution in a bottle with an eye dropper–type lid in the bathroom near my working area. I put a few drops of the bleach solution onto the middle of a 2" x 1" piece of the test fabric and watch the color discharge. . .or not. Wait about two minutes, rinse it out, and let it dry. You should see a difference in the color. If it hasn't discharged by then, it probably isn't going to. Some dyes discharge very quickly. Some dyes are more colorfast than others and take longer to discharge. Some never do.

Samples of discharged fabrics

No matter which fabric you choose, be sure to test a small sample before you begin your project.

I keep track of which fabrics in my stash will discharge by pinning or folding this small discharge sample into the corner of the yardage that it came from. This way, when I start a new project, I can immediately tell which fabrics will work for me without having to retest them.

Cut your background fabrics generously before you discharge, leaving at least several inches to spare in either direction. Don't skimp. The fabric will be washed and dried again after discharging, and you will lose a little to fraying along the sides, and maybe a little to additional shrinkage.

DISCHARGING CHEMICALS

Before you discharge any fabric, you'll need to collect a few chemicals. Some you may have around the house; others may be unfamiliar to you.

You need two kinds of chemicals to discharge the dye from fabric: one to remove the dye and the other to remove the dye remover.

Chlorine Bleach

Although chlorine bleach is a common household chemical, please treat it with respect. It is very dangerous. It's great at killing bacteria, and it's not so good for you either!

The Consumer Product Safety Commission has extensive regulations for labeling dangerous household products. You can tell how dangerous any given chemical is by the *signal words* on the label.

- "Caution" or "Warning:" Indicates a chronic hazard. These are dangerous products, but they will merely cause sickness or injury, as opposed to the ones labeled . . .
- "Danger:" These products are corrosive, flammable, and/or highly toxic. These are the very worst of the worst; they do irreversible damage.

Guess which one chlorine bleach is.

SAFETY PRECAUTIONS

PLEASE OBSERVE THESE SAFETY PRECAUTIONS WHENEVER YOU WORK WITH BLEACH.

- Discharge your fabrics outside, if possible. You need lots of air circulation, especially when you are spraying bleach. You should never spray bleach in a very fine mist unless you are wearing an adequate respirator with an acid gas cartridge. Do not spray bleach in a closed room.

- Wear old clothes and rubber gloves when working with bleach. And always keep yourself upwind from the bleach when spraying or splattering to avoid breathing the fumes or getting bleach on your clothes or skin. Immediately rinse off any bleach that comes in contact with your skin.

- Make a habit of rinsing your gloved hands often in a bucket of clear water as you work. This will help avoid accidental contact with the eyes or face, and it will also help avoid random discharge spots on your fabric.

- Resist the urge to hover over your creation while it is discharging; you really don't want to breathe the fumes. Keep a respectful distance.

Stop Bath

Chlorine will continue to eat away at your fabric unless it is chemically stopped. Just washing the fabric is not enough. There are several ways to stop the discharge process.

- Anti-chlor: The most reliable way to stop the bleach reaction is to use a product called Anti-chlor. It is available through PRO Chemical & Dye (see Resources). A teaspoon dissolved in 2½ gallons of warm water is all you need to make a stop bath.
- Hydrogen peroxide solution (available over the counter at any pharmacy or grocery store): Mix a solution of hydrogen peroxide and water, at the rate of 1 part hydrogen peroxide to 8–10 parts water.
- Vinegar: You can also use a solution of vinegar and water in roughly equal parts. This is the least effective stop bath.

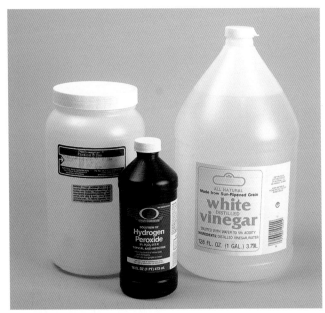

Stop Bath Products

The stop bath process is a batch process—that is, you use the bath once and then discard it. Add all your rinsed discharged fabrics to the bath at once, let them soak for five minutes (stirring occasionally), remove the fabric, and then discard the stop bath. The neutralizing chemicals have been used up. Make a new stop bath for the next batch of fabric.

Chlorine will continue to eat away at your fabric unless it is chemically stopped.

Have everything ready before you discharge.

Fabric discharged dry

Fabric discharged wet

Templates anchored on background fabric

DISCHARGING

Discharging is a quick process. It pays to have everything ready before you start.

Materials Needed

- ◼ Spray bottle containing a 50:50 solution of bleach and water
- ◼ A stop bath (see page 61)—enough to easily accommodate the amount of fabric that will be discharged
- ◼ Rubber gloves
- ◼ Newspapers and plastic drop cloth to cover your working area
- ◼ 2 buckets or tubs of clear water
- ◼ Prewashed fabric, generously cut
- ◼ Masks of the shapes you want to discharge
- ◼ Respirator with an acid gas canister if you have poor ventilation

Choose a calm day for discharging. It's hard to keep your fabric and masks anchored down when it's windy; plus, you really don't want a lot of bleach overspray.

Spread newspapers and plastic to protect the surface of your table or the ground and to provide a dry surface for the fabric.

Lay your prewashed fabric on the newspaper. You can discharge your fabric wet or dry. Wet fabric tends to spread out the bleach solution more, creating a softer, blurrier shadow and more even color in the background. Paper masks tend to curl up on wet fabric. Dry fabric has a crisper, dottier look to it, with sharper shadows, because the bleach solution tends to stay in droplets on the surface. Both methods provide very effective shadows. It's up to you.

Lay your masks on the fabric according to your design. Remember that we are placing the shadows here, not the appliqué pieces themselves. The shadows are slightly off to one side and lower than where the appliqué or fused pieces will go. You need to offset the masks according to your design. If you are randomly tossing your masks down (which is fine!), just remember that the shadows will be off to one side of your appliquéd pieces. Don't forget to allow for seam allowances, shrinkage, and fraying; give yourself some space from the edge of the fabric.

Anchor your masks if there is a breeze. I like to use pea gravel or other small stones, because I can put just enough on the masks that I don't accidentally cast a shadow of the rocks (and there are lots of rocks in my yard, so small rocks are always handy).

Put on your rubber gloves and respirator. Standing upwind from your fabric, spray the bleach solution at the fabric from a height of 12"–18". Do not circle your working area; spray from one spot. Imagine that you are the light source. The spray of bleach solution is the light streaming from you and casting shadows on the fabric. If you spray from other angles, you will change the illusion of your shadows. It's more effective to spray from one angle only.

Spray as much solution as your fabric needs to discharge. How much is that? It depends on your fabric, the weather, the strength of your bleach solution, and so on. Your fabric should be thoroughly dampened.

As soon as you have sprayed enough bleach solution, gently remove the masks, taking care

Spray fabric with bleach solution from one direction.

not to let them drip onto the fabric (although that can be an interesting effect in itself, and not necessarily a disaster). Try not to touch the fabric itself. Throw the masks away.

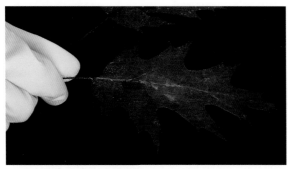
Remove leaf masks carefully.

Now you can see the dye discharging from your fabric. It is like watching a Polaroid picture develop. The shape of your masks will slowly (or quickly) appear on the surface of the fabric. It takes only a few minutes. It's very exciting!

Watch from a respectful distance. Try not to hover over the fabric, as there are a lot of chlorine fumes rising from it.

It takes a little experience to determine when the discharge process is "finished." Keep in mind that since the fabric is wet, the shapes are not as distinct as they will become once it is washed and dried.

When the shapes have "developed" as much as you want them to, plunge the fabric into a tub or bucket of clear water to rinse out the bulk of the bleach solution. I like to use a large plastic sweater box full of water, so that I can lay the fabric flat without scrunching or folding the fabric. It's easy for

Carefully lay the fabric in rinse water as flat as possible.

the bleach solution to "migrate" somewhere that you didn't intend to discharge. Pump the fabric up and down a few times in the water to really rinse it out. If you are discharging several pieces, you can keep your discharged fabrics in the rinse water until you are ready to use the stop bath.

If you spray too lightly
The good news:
- You're less likely to damage your fabric.

The bad news:
- You may not get a good discharge from your fabric.
- Shadows may not show up on your fabric.
- You've wasted your time and effort.

If you spray too heavily
The good news:
- You'll get a good discharge.

The bad news:
- You're more likely to damage your fabric.
- You may "overdischarge" your fabric, making it look too stark.
- You may overly blur the outline of your masks, making your shadows indistinct.
- Bleach solution may drip from the masks as you lift them, making unintentional discharge spots.

Try to find that balance. Don't start out discharging a yard of your favorite expensive hand-dyed fabric. Practice on some smaller pieces until you are comfortable with the process and results. It can be difficult to tell how much discharging has taken place until the fabric is washed and dried. You can ruin more fabric faster with discharging than any other process that I know of (short of fire, flood, and other total disasters).

When you are done discharging, move the rinsed fabrics to the stop bath. Plunge the fabric up and down a few times to really work the stop bath solution throughout the fibers. Let the fabric remain in the stop bath for five minutes or so, stirring it occasionally. Discard the exhausted stop bath solution.

When you have finished your discharge session, launder your discharged fabrics in the washing machine with a mild detergent.

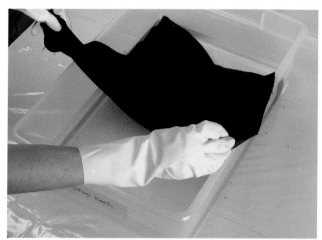

Move the fabric to the stop bath.

Discharged fabric

FINISHING YOUR DESIGN

Your shadowed background fabric is ready for the finishing touches. It's beautiful on its own. Sure—you can stop here if you want. But if you want a shadowed look, it's time for that fabric to meet its destiny—time to add your appliqué pieces!

Place appliqué leaves on shadows.

Lay out your appliqué pieces on your dry, ironed, discharged fabric. Find the shadow that corresponds to each piece. Place each piece slightly higher and to one side of its shadow.

Now stand back and have a look. Are the shadows behind the pieces convincing you that the composition looks three-dimensional? Try to maintain a consistent angle of placement. This helps convince you that there is a single light source that could cast shadows like that. Maintaining a consistent distance from the shadows also helps. You may have to do a little tweaking here and there to make the composition look right.

When you have nudged your pieces into a satisfying configuration—hurray! If you are fusing, go ahead and press them down according to the manufacturer's instructions. You're done! If you are hand or machine appliquéing, pin or baste the pieces into place—and get busy sewing!

WISE TIP I find a reducing lens a very useful tool for this step. A reducing lens is the opposite of a magnifying glass—it makes things look far away. You can buy one at your local quilt shop. Or you can buy a door peephole at your local hardware store (just make sure it isn't too distorting). Or you can look through the back end of a pair of binoculars. A reducing lens allows me to keep my work at arm's length while giving me a vision of it from across the room.

Botanically Correct

A wreath of leaves appears to float on the surface of this simple quilt. Careful discharging of the background fabric to create the illusion of shadows makes this quilt look three-dimensional.

Botanically Correct, 24½" x 24½"

BEFORE YOU START

Be sure to read the safety precautions (page 60) before starting this project!

Prewash all fabrics. Flatten 5–7 simple leaves such as oaks, maples, and so on, in a phone book for a few days, or make 5 paper cutout copies of the leaf pattern given here.

Part of the charm of using actual leaves is the variation found in nature. No two leaves are exactly alike. I recommend using actual leaves whenever possible. However, if it's the dead of winter, or you live in the Sahara Desert or on the tundra, you can trace this leaf pattern to use.

MATERIALS AND SUPPLIES

Background: 1 fat quarter dark solid fabric (Pretest your fabric to be sure it discharges!)

Border: ½ yard

Leaves: Scraps of 5 bright fabrics

Paper-backed fusible web: ½ yard

Discharging materials:
- Spray bottle of a 50:50 solution of bleach and water
- Stop bath
- Rubber gloves
- Newspapers and plastic drop cloth to cover your working area
- 2 buckets or tubs of clear water
- Respirator

5 simple leaves: flattened or 5 paper cut-outs of the leaf pattern

Backing: 1 yard

Batting: 28" x 28"

Binding: ½ yard

CUTTING

Background
- Leave the fat quarter untrimmed until after the discharging process.

Border
- Cut 4 strips 4" x fabric width.

PREPARE FUSIBLE LEAVES

1. Using the leaves as templates, trace around each leaf, **right side down,** on paper-backed fusible web.

Oak leaf pattern

 WISE TIP You will need to match up your fabric leaves with their corresponding shadows when you are done discharging. Sometimes it can be hard to figure out which leaf goes with which shadow when you are looking at your discharged fabric. To help match shadow to leaf when I'm done, I like to number my leaves in the order that they will lay on the fabric. I actually write the number on the back of the leaf with an indelible marker, with corresponding numbers on the fusible web.

2. Roughly cut out each fusible leaf. Do not cut out the leaves neatly yet; just separate them.

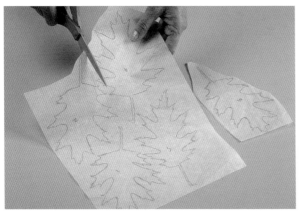

Separate the fusible leaves.

3. Iron the fusible web leaves to the wrong side of bright fabrics as desired. Follow the manufacturer's instructions for fusible web.

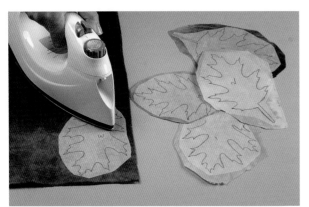

Iron the fusible leaves to bright fabrics.

4. Cut out the fused leaves carefully along your marked lines.

Cut out the fusible leaves.

DISCHARGE BACKGROUND FABRIC

Follow the discharging procedure described in this chapter (pages 62–64).

1. Follow the safety instructions in this chapter!

2. Protect your working surface with newspapers and plastic. Wear rubber gloves.

3. Prepare the bleach solution and stop bath.

4. Lay the background fabric flat on newspapers. The background fabric may be wet or dry.

5. Place leaves, **right side up**, on the background fabric. Arrange your leaves in a pleasant circle. Anchor them down if there is any kind of breeze. Be sure that your anchors will not cast unwanted shadows on the fabric.

6. Spray bleach solution from one direction.

7. Remove the leaves carefully.

8. Watch leaves the "develop."

9. When the fabric is as discharged as you want it, rinse it carefully in clear water.

10. Lay the fabric in the stop bath, and let the fabric soak in the bath for 5 minutes, stirring occasionally.

11. Wash with mild detergent, dry, and iron as usual. It's beautiful!

Discharged fabric

ADD LEAVES TO BACKGROUND

1. Match the leaves to the corresponding shadows on the background fabric. Each leaf is a little different and needs to get back with its own shadow. The bleach bleeds around the edges a little bit, so the shadows are a little smaller than the actual leaves.

2. Remove the paper backing from the fused leaves.

3. Place the leaves on the background fabric with their corresponding shadows. Start by placing the leaves directly over their shadows. Now move each leaf up and to the right of its shadow. Try to maintain a consistent angle and distance. Use a reducing lens or step back from your work. Do the leaves look like they are floating?

4. Press the leaves to the background according to the fusible web manufacturer's instructions.

Leaves are fused to fabric.

5. Trim the background fat quarter to approximately 18" x 18". Center the fused wreath motif, not the shadows. The actual size of the background piece is not critical. Do what is best for your quilt; cut it to the size that looks best on your piece.

QUILT CONSTRUCTION

1. Measure the quilt through the center vertically to calculate the length of the side borders. Cut 2 border strips to this measurement and sew them to the sides of the quilt. Press the seams toward the border.

2. Measure the quilt (plus side borders) through the center horizontally to calculate the length of the top and bottom borders. Cut 2 border strips to this measurement and sew them to the top and bottom of the quilt. Press the seams toward the border.

QUILTING AND FINISHING

1. Layer and baste the quilt top, batting, and backing.

2. Quilt by hand or machine using your preferred design, or quilt in the ditch.

3. Block the quilt. Lay out the quilt on a large horizontal surface such as the floor. Smooth the quilt into shape. Steam the quilt with a steam iron until damp. Allow the quilt to dry completely, (usually overnight), before picking it up.

4. Bind.

Chapter Six

Remember the good old days. So let's go back there! Let's give ourselves the gift of a new set of crayons and some blank paper and the time to just play. We'll apply our new knowledge about depth and dimension to old familiar concepts of coloring and painting, and combine it all with fabric and quilting.

It's fun to play on fabric with oil sticks and oil pastels. You can add dimension with shadows, as we have been doing so far with piecing, appliqué, and discharge. Placement? No problem! Just paint on shadows wherever you want them. Color? No need to shop for that perfect shadow fabric—just mix your own. If in doubt—use gray.

PRODUCTS

There are many products for marking on fabric—acrylics, oil bars and pastels, thickened dyes, fabric markers, watercolor crayons and pastels, inks. If you have a favorite medium, use it. I'll discuss my favorites briefly.

Acrylic Paints

There is a wide range of acrylic paints that can be used for painting on fabric. They range from the inexpensive 2-ounce bottles of liquid acrylics found at all craft stores (Ceramcoat, for example) to jars of thick pudding-like silk-screening paint (Versatex fabric paint). I recommend Setacolor, which is a nice liquid acrylic that leaves a fairly soft hand on the fabric.

Acrylic paints can be opaque; that is, they completely cover the color of the fabric underneath. To make your acrylic shadows more convincing, thin the acrylic paint with water to make the shadows more transparent. This makes the paint runny. Be sure to blot your brush; don't try to paint a shadow with a fully loaded, drippy brush. The brush should be nearly dry.

Acrylic paint should be allowed to dry and then heat set with a hot iron.

Oil Bars (or Sticks) and Oil Pastels

Hands down, oil bars or pastels are my favorite tools for shading and shadowing on fabric. I like the control the oils afford me. They are so easy to blend and feather, even for the artistically challenged (like me). I can create a soft, air-brushed look with them. I like the easy set-up and general cleanliness of the process (no water, no slop). I can use them in the family room while I watch a movie. I can travel with them without worrying that they might leak. I use the same colors so often, and use so little actual paint, that I don't even bother cleaning out my brushes. I just stick 'em in little recloseable plastic bags.

Remember back in kindergarten—those fat crayons, that big blank sheet of newsprint? Or those cups of tempera paint and big fat brushes?

Use good-quality acrylic paint.

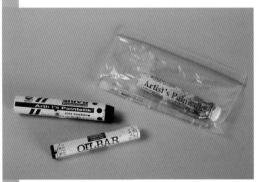

Oil bars or sticks

Oil pastels

Oil bars (or oil sticks, as they are sometimes called) and oil pastels are different—and yet the same. They are both made of pigments (powdered color) bound with oil and a bit of wax. What's the difference?

- Oil bars are bound with linseed oil. Linseed oil is a "drying oil"; like oil-based paint, it will dry to a tough flexible film when applied thickly. It dries on the surface of the oil bar itself as well, which means that you have to scrape off this dried film of oil to get to the soft stick underneath. I use an X-ACTO knife to peel off this thin skin.

- Oil pastels are bound with mineral oil. Mineral oil is a "non-drying oil"; it never dries out. That means that on any oil pastel painting, you will always be able to smear the paint. This is not such a big deal on fabric, because we can heat set the pigment into the fabric, and smearing won't be much of an issue. Oil pastels are ready to use right out of the box; no skin to peel off.

My generic favorite shadow color is called Payne's gray. It's almost black, but not as stark, and it has a blue cast to it that mimics shadows.

NOTE: I don't worry too much about damage from linseed or mineral oil. Artists paint a "ground," or primer, all over their canvases before painting to protect them from the oil paint—but that's not an option with a quilt. I counter that the risk of damage is low because I use the paint so sparingly on the surface that the exposure is minimal compared to the exposure for a painting. I could also wash my painted fabrics to remove the oil (although the color degrades somewhat with washing, more so with the pastels than the oil bars).

	ADVANTAGES	DISADVANTAGES
Acrylics	Clean up with soap and water. Better-quality paints are archival, lightfast, and safe for fabrics. Colors can be mixed easily to customize the color you need. Can be thinned with water to produce a transparent "wash" of color.	Can affect the hand of the fabric, especially the cheaper acrylics, which can make the fabric hard to quilt through and stiff to the touch. Blending colors into the fabric for shading is a little more challenging for the artistically impaired.
Oil Bars or Sticks	Permanent and lightfast. Creamy and oh-so-easy to blend. Colors are intense for the amount of paint applied. It takes only a little! Leave no stiffness on the fabric.	Color range is limited (but they can be blended to create specific colors). Hard to find, even at retail art supply stores (but they can be found easily online). Linseed oil is not archival. See note at left. Clean up with solvents.
Oil pastels	Large variety of colors. Even the highest-quality pastels are fairly inexpensive. Leave no stiffness on the fabric.	Not as creamy and easy to blend as oil bars. Colors are not as intense as oil bars, especially on dark fabrics. Mineral oil is not archival. See note at left. Clean up with solvents.

How to Use Oil Bars and Pastels

Oil bars and pastels are pretty concentrated for our use in shading and shadowing. We need only a "blush" of paint on the surface of the quilt. We're only trying to make a shadow, after all, not change the color itself; the color is already in the fabric. If we apply the oil bars directly to the fabric, we'll have too much color, and we won't be able to blend it easily. We'll have more control if we apply the paint indirectly, with a brush.

A bit of waxed paper makes a great palette. We can lay down paint and mix colors on it, and when we are done, we can clean up with a crumple.

Materials

- ■ Oil bars or pastels
- ■ Fabric
- ■ Waxed paper
- ■ Stencil brush, medium (or cotton-tipped swabs or an old toothbrush)

1. Rub the oil bar or pastel on the waxed paper to cover an area roughly 1" x 1".

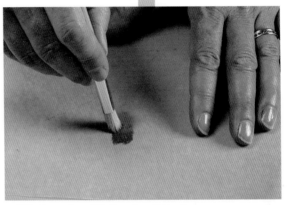

2. Lift the paint with the stencil brush.

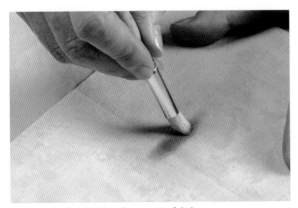

3. Rub the loaded brush on your fabric.

4. Mix colors on your disposable palette.

It's that simple. You can feather and blend this paint to create a soft air-brushed look. Experiment with the paint on some scraps of fabric to get a feel for the medium before you start on your first quilting project.

You can blend colors on the waxed paper. For example, if you need a burgundy color but don't have one, you can create that color by painting black and red next to each other on your waxed paper palette. Pick up both colors at once with your stencil brush to mix them together, and then apply the mixed paint to the fabric. You can mix as many colors as you like.

Good practice suggests that if you are using oil bars, you should allow your painted fabric to "cure" for a few days before heat setting. This allows the oils in the paint to react with the air and harden. Theoretically, the oil paint can bleed and leave an oily mark on your fabric if it hasn't cured properly. In reality, I can rarely wait that long. I find it hard to wait much more than an hour sometimes, and I haven't had any problems with bleeding. However, I do use the paint very sparingly. There's very little oil involved.

CREATING PUDDLED SHADOWS WITH PAINT

Puddled shadows are those blurry, blobby shadows under many three-dimensional objects (pages 11–12). Picture a tree on a golf course and the shadow it casts—that's a puddled shadow. It's easy to create puddled shadows with paint. You don't have to be an "artist" to rub a little paint on fabric and make a convincing shadow.

There are just a few rules about puddled shadows:

■ The width of the shadow should be equal to or greater than the width of the object itself. Picture a basket of flowers. If the sun is directly overhead, this object will cast a shadow that is as wide as the widest point of the basket plus flowers. If the sun is lower in the sky (morning or afternoon), the shadow will be wider than the basket plus flowers, and it will be off-center.

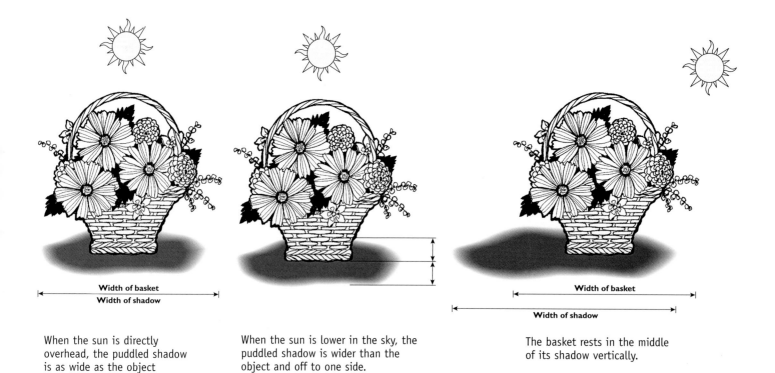

Width of basket
Width of shadow

Width of basket

Width of shadow

When the sun is directly overhead, the puddled shadow is as wide as the object

When the sun is lower in the sky, the puddled shadow is wider than the object and off to one side.

The basket rests in the middle of its shadow vertically.

An object at rest should sit about in the middle of its puddled shadow vertically. This placement makes the object look anchored to the ground. If the object is placed too high above its puddled shadow, it looks as if it's hovering in midair, which may not be the effect you are trying to achieve. A reducing lens can be helpful when placing your object on its puddled shadow.

A ball casts a neat lens-shaped shadow.

Regular-shaped objects cast fairly regular shadows. For example, a ball casts a shadow that looks like a neat and regular lens shape, thicker in the middle and tapering out at each end. An irregular object (that basket of flowers) casts an irregular shadow. Its shadow can be just a blurry blob. It's hard to go wrong. If the basket has a lot of flowers that stick out at odd angles you might want to try to have a bumpy shadow, but otherwise, a blurry blob works amazingly well.

Paint your puddled shadows on your background before placing your appliqué pieces. Although you can always go back and add shadows later if you want, it's easier and freer to paint if there are not a lot of pieces to mask off.

Gravity detail (full quilt page 110). Technique: puddled shadows

- Mark the shadow area lightly on the background. Use an easy-to-remove marker such as chalk.

- Load your brush with shadow-colored paint. Starting in the center of the shadow, apply the paint lightly to the background, working back and forth out to the edges as the brush becomes drier. The center of the shadow will be its darkest point. When your brush is dry, use it to feather the edges of the shadow to give them a realistic blurry look.

- Allow the paint to dry if you are using acrylics. If you are using oil bars, it's good to allow the paint to cure for up to three days.

- Finish by heat setting the paint. Press the fabric with your iron at a high setting, using a press cloth to protect your iron.

- Add your appliqué pieces to the shadowed background. Be sure to place your objects at the appropriate place in their shadows.

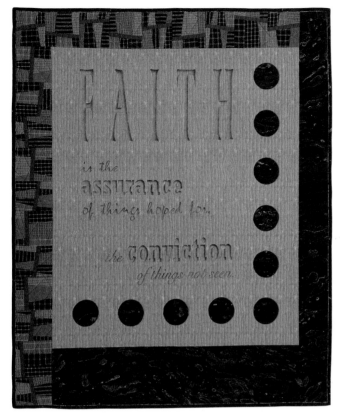

Hebrews 11:1, 51" x 42"

CREATING IMPLIED SHAPES WITH PAINT

By using shading, we can *imply* a shape that is not actually there. This occurred to me one day as I was walking through a cemetery. I noticed that the carving on the headstones was not a different color from the rest of the granite; the way the light fell on the carving made the words visible. The light creates both a shine and a shadow. We can re-create that shading with paint on fabric.

We can imply shapes two different ways: We can *emboss* them or we can *engrave* them. Embossing looks like it sticks *out* of the surface (as on a nice business card); engraving looks carved *into* the surface (as on a nice tombstone).

Whether we are embossing or engraving, we'll use two colors: white and shadow. *White* will indicate where the light is reflected on the material, and *shadow* will indicate the shaded surfaces. Shadow color can be a darker, duller shade of the background fabric; or it can be a generic dark gray color. As I mentioned, my favorite generic shadow color is Payne's gray.

Engraving

Engraving is carved *into* the background material. The shadows fall *inside* the carving.

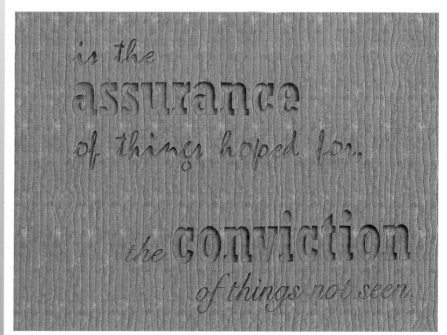

Engraving. In *Hebrews 11:1*, I was trying to give the effect of the words being carved into wood.

To engrave a shape, we'll use a stencil. A stencil is a hole to be filled in; it is the negative space, leaving the positive space visible.

You can use existing stencils, if you have them, or you can create our own. There are some beautiful plastic stencils available in quilt shops, online, and in the craft stores. They have the advantage of being washable and reusable.

Most of the time, I am making something specific for a particular quilt. I plan to use the stencil only once, maybe twice, so I like to make stencils from freezer paper. It's inexpensive, versatile, and easy to cut. It's also fairly large, so I can make a big image. I can draw or trace directly onto it. I can also manipulate text or images in my computer and then print directly onto 8½" x 11" sheets of freezer paper, taping them together as needed.

1. Cut the freezer paper stencil with an X-ACTO knife or with scissors. Using an X-ACTO knife has the benefit of leaving the mask intact—you can save it for another project.

2. Position the stencil in place on your background fabric. You can tape it in place if it's a plastic stencil, or iron it in place if it's freezer paper.

To create an engraving, first decide on the location and direction of your light source. Light will shine on the edges of the stencil that are farthest from the light, and shadows will fall where the edge of the stencil is closest to the light. Let's assume that your light source is in the upper right corner of the quilt. Light will shine on the lower left edges of the stencil, and shadows will fall on the upper right edges of the stencil. We'll add white paint where the light is shining, and shadow paint where the shadows fall.

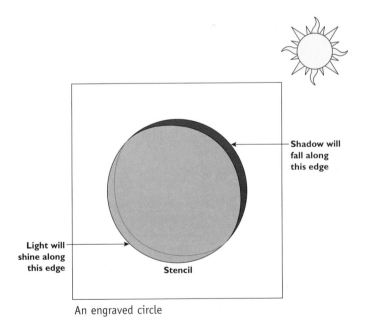

Light will shine along this edge

Shadow will fall along this edge

Stencil

An engraved circle

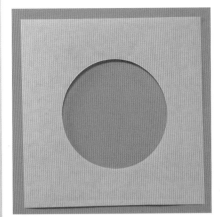

Stencil

WISE TIP You can load your brush in the usual way, but when I'm using oil bars or pastels, I'm kind of lazy and I like to skip that step. I still apply the paint indirectly, with a brush, but I draw directly on the edge of the stencil with the oil bar or pastel and then brush the paint from the stencil onto the fabric. Draw a heavier line where you want more paint; lighter where you want less. Use a stencil brush to brush the paint toward the fabric. Add a bit more here and there as needed to create a smooth, uniform shadow or shine.

Add paint directly on the stencil.

Brush the paint toward the fabric.

Shine will be widest at this point

Stencil

Add the shine first with white paint.

Shadow will be widest at this point

Stencil

Add the shadow last.

3. Start with the white paint. Add a "shine" to the lower left edges of all your stencils. This is where the light will shine, because that edge of the engraving is oriented toward the light. Brush the white paint about ½" into the stencil toward the light source. The "shine" will be widest where the stencil edge is closest to perpendicular to the light source, and will taper off toward the areas where the edge of the stencil is parallel to the direction of the light.

4. Once you have added all the "shine," you can add the "shadow." The process is the same, only exactly the opposite. Brush the shadow paint about ½" into the stencil in the *opposite* direction of the light source. The shadow will be widest where the edge of the stencil is closest to perpendicular to the direction of the light, and will taper off toward the areas where the edge of the stencil is parallel to the direction of the light. At these points, the shine and shadow converge. Blend the two paints to blur them where they meet.

5. Remove the stencils and have a look. You've engraved something!

Embossing

Embossing sticks *out* from the background. The shadows fall *outside* the embossing. The object itself is not changed in color or shading, just the area immediately surrounding it.

This banner was made for the back of our upright piano at church. The word "Jesus" was torn from freezer paper and used as a mask to create the look of a raised surface.

To emboss a shape, we'll use a mask. A mask is a shape, a positive space that leaves the negative space visible around it.

Masks are the opposite of stencils; a mask is the actual shape of an object (whereas a stencil is a hole in the shape of an object). Masks are a little tougher to come by in the stores than stencils are. That's okay because masks are easier to cut out than stencils, and we can cut our own.

I like to make masks from freezer paper, just like stencils. Masks are easy to cut out with scissors because we are cutting a positive shape rather than cutting a hole as we were with the stencils. Again, you can trace or draw directly onto the freezer paper, or print images or text from your computer onto 8½" x 11" sheets of freezer paper. Sometimes I even tear the freezer paper to create a mask. Torn freezer paper makes an interesting deckle edge.

1. To create an embossing, first decide on the location and direction of your light source. The shine and shadows on the embossing will be the opposite of those on the engraving. Light will shine on the edges of the mask that are *closest* to the light, and shadows will fall where the edges of the mask are *farthest* from the light. Let's assume that your light source is in the upper right corner of the quilt. Shadows will fall on the lower left edges of the mask, and light will shine on the upper right edges of the mask.

Mask

Torn freezer paper creates a deckle edge.

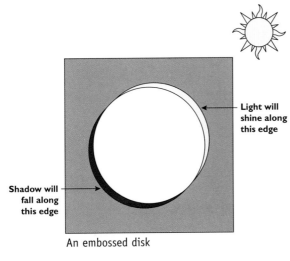

Light will shine along this edge

Shadow will fall along this edge

An embossed disk

2. Position the mask in place on your fabric. If it's freezer paper, iron it in place. If it's a plastic mask, you can tape it in place using double-faced tape on the underside of the mask. Note that any tape along the edge of the mask will interfere with the painted edge. If you're confident, you can just hold it in place.

3. Start with the white paint. Add a "shine" to the upper right edges of all your masks. This is where the light will shine, because that edge of the "embossing" is oriented toward the light. Load your brush in the usual way, or draw directly along the edge of the mask. Draw a heavier line where you want more paint, lighter where you want less.

4. Brush the paint from the mask onto the fabric.

> **WISE TIP**
> If an engraved or embossed object is shiny, it will have both shine and shadow (and you'll use both white and shadow-colored paints). But if the object has a more matte finish, it may not "shine" at all. In that case, skip the white paint and brush a very small amount of shadow paint on the shiny side of the object, just to mark its outline.

Detail of embossing technique

Draw directly on the mask.

Brush the paint toward the fabric in the direction of the light.

5. Brush the white paint about ½" away from the mask toward the light. The "shine" will be widest where the mask edge is closest to perpendicular to the light source, and will taper off toward the areas where the edge of the mask is parallel to the direction of the light.

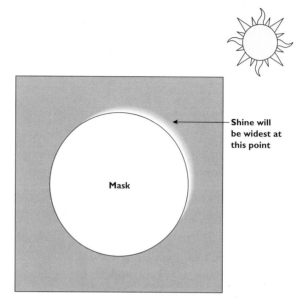

Add the shine with white paint first.

6. Once you have added all the "shine," you can add the "shadow." Brush the shadow paint about ½" away from the mask in the *opposite* direction of the light. The shadow will be widest where the edge of the mask is closest to perpendicular to the direction of the light, and will taper off toward the areas where the edges of the mask are parallel to the direction of the light. At these parallel points, the shine and shadow converge. Blend the two paints to blur them where they meet.

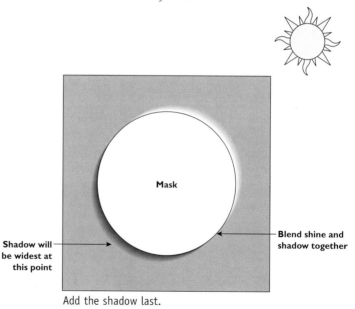

Add the shadow last.

7. Remove the mask and have a look. Your embossed object should be "outstanding"!

CREATING SHADOWED SHAPES WITH PAINT

We can also add shadows to individual fused or appliquéd shapes using paint. The shadows give the shape the appearance of being raised above the surface of the background.

Handspan detail. Each of the individual hands in the edge blocks was shadowed to create a little bit of depth.

Handspan, 39" x 39". Techniques: pieced shadows, painted shadowed shapes.

Shadowing a shape is basically the same as embossing. The difference is that embossing *implies* a shape: There is nothing actually there. This time, we'll fill in that implied area with a fused or appliquéd shape.

The instructions for creating a shadowed shape are the same as for embossing, with one additional step.

1. Decide on the direction of your light source.

2. Cut out your masks. They will be *exactly* the same shape as the appliqué or fused pieces you wish to shadow.

3. Position your masks on the background fabric.

4. Add white paint along the light edges of each mask (closest to the light source).

5. Add shadow paint along the dark edges of each mask (farthest from the light source). Remove the masks and allow the paint to dry or cure. Heat set the paint.

6. Add the appliqué piece. This piece should fit perfectly within the boundaries of the paint.

It can be challenging to cut two shapes *exactly* the same: a freezer paper mask *and* an appliqué pattern piece. Even if you are cutting out simple shapes like circles, there are bound to be tiny slivers of unpainted fabric here and there that show through when you fit your piece into the shadow boundaries you have set.

If you are appliquéing by hand or machine, you can make small adjustments in the seam allowance to cover those show-through spots. Fusing is more unforgiving. You just can't stretch a too small piece to cover a bigger area.

I can't claim to be a Van Gogh or even a Pollack, but I can still create some cool effects with paint. You can too!

Cut your freezer paper mask while you cut out your fused shapes. The shiny side of the freezer paper is against the fabric.

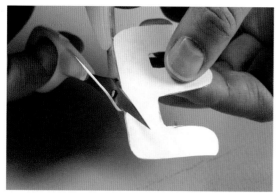

Shave off the edges of your freezer paper mask.

Peel off the backing paper from your pattern piece and use the paper for a mask

WISE TIPS Here are some tips for all you fusers out there.

- When you cut out a fused fabric piece, hold a piece of freezer paper with it and cut out both of them at the same time. Make sure that the shiny side of the freezer paper is against the fabric side of the fused piece, so that the mask is not a mirror image of the piece.

- Cut your freezer paper mask *slightly smaller* than the fused piece. Shave off just a bit all along the edge of each mask. That way, if the fused piece is not exactly the same, you won't have an unpainted sliver of fabric showing between the piece and its shadow. Don't make the mask too small though—not more than about ⅛". You run the risk of seeing the paint under the edge of the fused piece.

- Best tip last: Don't even bother with freezer paper masks. Just cut out your shapes from your fused fabric, peel off the backing paper from the fusible web, and use this *backing paper* for your masks. Why not? It's the *exact* shape of your fused piece of fabric, down to every last scissor mark. You just have to be extra careful when using them as masks, because they are not anchored to the fabric. You could use double-faced tape, or you could pin them in place. But you'll still have to hold them very carefully as you brush the paint around them. Be sure to use the correct side of the backing paper, so that you don't paint the mirror image of your piece. The correct side to use is the side that was touching the fabric, not the side that you drew your pattern on.

Fusers have the advantage of being able to heat set their paint as they apply their pieces.

Square Peg, Round Hole

Square pegs in round holes in squares. That's this quilt. The circles aren't really there, are they? We'll use a freezer paper mask and fabric paint to imply circles on our squares. Then we'll fill them with square pegs!

Square Peg, Round Hole, 31½" x 31½"

BEFORE YOU START

You can fuse or appliqué (by hand or machine) the center squares.

The paint choice is up to you. I've used oil sticks for this project, but other types of paint will work as well.

MATERIALS AND SUPPLIES

Checkerboard:

- ½ yard dark
- ½ yard red

Central squares: ¼ yard yellow

Border: ¾ yard of dark

Paper-backed fusible web: ¼ yard, if you are fusing the yellow squares

Freezer paper

Oil sticks, pastels, or acrylic paints: white and black

Stencil brushes: 2

Backing: 1 yard

Batting: 36" x 36"

Binding: ¼ yard

CUTTING

Checkerboard:

- Dark: Cut 2 strips 5" x fabric width; then cut the strips into 12 squares, 5" x 5".
- Red: Cut 2 strips 5" x fabric width; then cut the strips into 13 squares, 5" x 5".
- Yellow squares: If you are appliquéing by hand or machine, cut 2 strips 2" x fabric width; then cut the strips into 25 squares, 2" x 2". If you are fusing, leave the yellow yardage whole.
- Border: Cut 4 strips 5" x fabric width.

CONSTRUCTION
Round Holes

1. Cut several 3" circle masks from freezer paper using the pattern on page 83. You can use the same circle several times; be sure to protect your iron with a pressing cloth or paper towel from the paint on the mask if you are using the same mask again.

2. Iron a freezer paper circle mask to the center of a 5" dark square. Brush white paint around the edge of the circle using a clean stencil brush. The upper right edge of the circle should have the most paint (extending about ½" beyond the mask at the widest point), because this is the "brightest" side of the circle. The lower left corner should have very little paint, just enough to define the circle.

3. Repeat 11 times, for a total of 12 dark squares.

Applying the white paint

4. Iron a fresh circle mask to the center of a 5" red square. Brush black paint around the edge of the circle using a stencil brush. The upper right edge of the circle should be barely painted, and the lower left edge of the circle should have the most paint (up to ½" away from the circle). The lower left edge is the "darkest" part of the circle's shadow.

5. Repeat 12 times, for a total of 13 red squares.

Applying the black paint

6. Allow the paint to dry, and heat set it with a hot iron.

Square Pegs

Appliqué by hand or machine the 2" yellow squares to the centers of each circle block. Finished appliquéd square size is 1½".

OR

Iron an 8" square piece of paper-backed fusible web to the back of the yellow fabric, following the manufacturer's instructions. Peel off the backing paper. Trim the edges. Cut 25 squares, 1½" x 1½", from the fused yellow fabric. Fuse one square into the center of each circle block.

QUILT CONSTRUCTION

1. Lay out the blocks on your design wall, alternating red and dark blocks. Be sure your painted circles are oriented correctly with respect to the implied light source.

2. Sew the blocks together into rows horizontally. Press the seams toward the dark fabric.

3. Sew the rows together, matching seams. Press the seams in one direction.

4. Measure the quilt through the center vertically to calculate the length of the side borders. Cut 2 border strips to this measurement and sew them to the sides of the quilt, easing if necessary. Press the seams toward the border.

5. Measure the quilt (plus side borders) through the center horizontally to calculate the length of the top and bottom borders. Cut 2 border strips to this measurement and sew them to the top and bottom of quilt, easing if necessary. Press the seams toward the border.

QUILTING AND FINISHING

1. Layer and baste the quilt top, batting, and backing.

2. Quilt by hand or machine along the edge of the painted circle. Additional quilting design is up to you.

3. Block the quilt. Lay out the quilt on a large horizontal surface such as the floor. Smooth the quilt into shape. Steam the quilt with a steam iron until damp. Allow the quilt to dry completely, (usually overnight), before picking it up.

4. Bind.

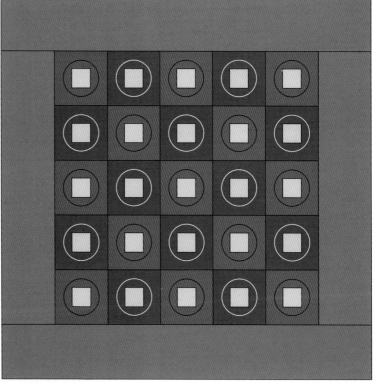

Quilt construction

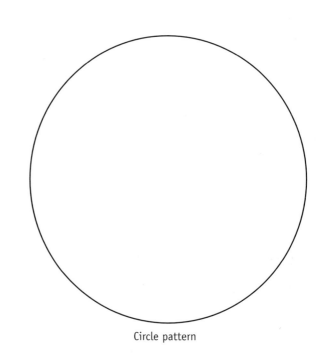

Circle pattern

No matter how many tools we may collect (or how few), there are always a few standbys that we reach for over and over again.

Color and value, piecing, appliqué, discharge, and painting are the big tools in my creative toolbox. They are the tools that I use most often to create a feeling of depth in my work. But beneath these stalwarts are a few minor tools that, every once in a while, come in handy. These minor tools are things like quilting, couching, and stamping. They may not get used everyday, but sometimes they are just the perfect tool for the job.

QUILTING

It's never too late to add a little shadowing! Quilting can emphasize shadows that you have already designed into the quilt top, or it can be added to create new shadows at the last minute.

When I am quilting a quilt top, I try to choose quilting designs that will emphasize the depth I have already created in my design. Sometimes the design of the quilt top is so bold that no extra emphasis is necessary; I need to do only minimal quilting. Stitching in the ditch may be all a quilt needs to maintain the excitement of the piece—anything else would be a distraction.

Boxes and Beyond, 49" x 43".
Stitching in the ditch keeps the focus on the dimensionality of this piece

When you are quilting directly on top of a pieced, appliquéd, painted, or discharged shadow, it's a good idea to match the color of your quilting thread to the shadow. Shadows aren't really a place to showcase your quilting skills with grand quilting designs or showy threads. They should be matte and mysterious. Shadows should try to remain in the background . . . seen and not heard.

Sometimes I need to add extra quilting to help a quilt lay flat, or to even out the amount of quilting over the surface of the quilt. Everything gets quilted heavily: the blocks, the background, even the shadowing.

Other times a little extra oomph needs to be added to the shadows (or the background) to bring out the three-dimensionality of the design. The shadows may be more subtle than desired. Thoughtful quilting can help strengthen a weak shadow. To emphasize shadows that are too faint or subtle, try quilting the shadows with dark thread, darker than the shadow fabric itself. Quilt the background area with a lighter thread for more contrast. And be sure to quilt heavily to make an impact.

Alder detail (full quilt page 35). Lots of quilting everywhere was needed to help this uncooperative quilt lie flat.

Gold Leaf, 37" x 37". Techniques: painted shadows, foiling, quilting.

Gold Leaf detail. The quilting enhances the subtle shadows of the leaves.

You can even add shadows that were never there—although shadowing with quilting is a little like putting on roll-on deodorant with a ballpoint pen. It's a fine tool for a big job. Quilting is not often my first choice for creating depth if I want a great impact, but it can be a great enhancement. Suppose you want to add a little depth to an element of your quilt design. You haven't pieced, appliquéd, or painted a shadow there, but you would like to add a little interest and dimension. It's not too late! You can still add a shadow by using a dark thread in the quilting. Quilt heavily along the edges you would like to shadow. The combination of the heavy quilting, which physically depresses the area around it, and the darker thread, which visually darkens the whole area it covers, can create a subtle shadow when viewed from a distance.

Mark your shadow area with chalk or other easily removed marking tool. Quilt back and forth to fill in the area, using a thread that is a darker shade of the background. Your quilting lines can run parallel to the edge of the shadow (like tight echo quilting), or they can be at a diagonal in the direction of the light source.

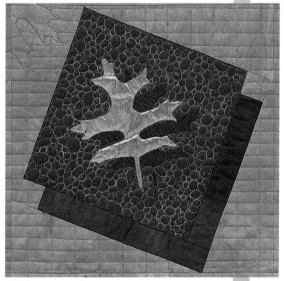

Gold Leaf detail.

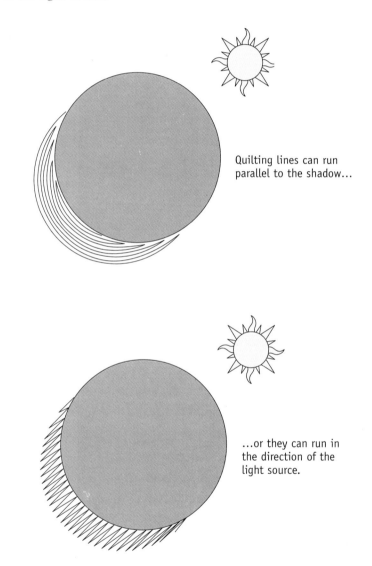

Quilting lines can run parallel to the shadow...

...or they can run in the direction of the light source.

The main thing to keep in mind is that you want to create an impact.

- Use a heavier-weight thread.
- Quilt heavily.

COUCHING

There are some gorgeous threads and yarns on the market today, and it's fun to showcase these on your quilt. If a thread is fine enough to go through the eye of your needle, or through the bobbin case, you can quilt directly with the decorative thread. But if the thread is too heavy—or if it is a yarn or ribbon—you can couch it on the surface of your quilt.

Couching is the easiest of all embellishments. It's simply applying a yarn to the surface by machine with a zigzag stitch. A cording or piping foot holds the yarn in place as you sew and makes keeping the zigzag stitch centered on the yarn easy. It also makes turning corners or following curves a cinch.

A *piping foot* has a single hole for the couching yarn. It's usually a good-size hole for a reasonably thick yarn or cord. A *cording foot* has a ridge of little teeth that can accommodate from three to seven smaller-diameter yarns.

A piping foot holds decorative yarn in place while you sew.

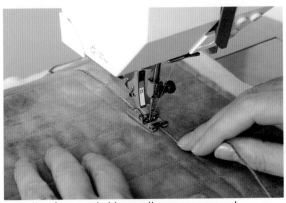

A cording foot can hold a smaller yarn or several decorative yarns at the same time.

Couching can be done either before or during your quilting. You can use any thread you like for your zigzag. Some people like to use invisible thread; others like to match the thread to the yarn they are couching; still others like to create a contrast between yarn and thread. It's up to you.

There are some gorgeous threads and yarns on the market today, and it's fun to showcase these on your quilt.

Shadowing a Line

Couching is easy. Now let's "float" those couched lines by adding a *second* line of quilting or couching, parallel to the couched yarn, using a shadow color such as gray or black. The principle is the same as when we added shadows to blocks or objects; we're just applying it to lines now. It can make the couched lines float.

SLIGHTLY FLOATING LINE

If the shadow is close to the couched yarn, it gives the line of couching a slight "lift," as if the line were hovering just slightly above the surface of the quilt.

Lighthouses, 40" x 36". Technique: shadowed couch-

Lighthouses detail. The variegated yarn is shadowed with a black line.

Leave a gap between the decorative yarn and the shadow yarn.

The shadow line can be couched at the same time as the decorative yarn itself using a cording foot. Leave a gap between the decorative yarn and the shadow yarn by skipping one or more "teeth" in your cording foot. Use invisible thread to help hide the fact that they have been couched together. And use an overcasting stitch (three stitches per zigzag) to lock the yarns in place, so they don't migrate.

HIGHER-FLYING LINE

If your line of decorative yarn is hovering higher than just barely off the surface, you may not be able to couch the decorative yarn and the shadow line at the same time. The shadows will fall farther away from the yarn, or they may fall onto elements of the design. You will have to couch these lines separately.

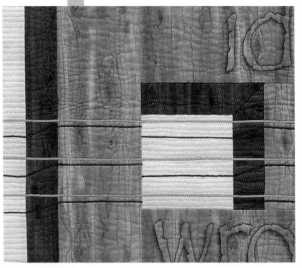

Marriage Quilt detail. The gold cord is shadowed with a line of gray yarn. The shadow goes up and over elements of the design.

Marriage Quilt, 57" x 44". Techniques: pieced shadows, perspective setting, shadowed couching.

Following a shadow means going up and over things that it falls on. Picture the shadow of a power line on a sunny day. The power line is basically straight, but the shadow of the power line goes up and over cars, bikes, people, curbs, and anything else that is directly underneath it. Unless there is nothing under the power line but a nice smooth road, its shadow is anything but straight.

The shadow of a couched line is the same. If its shadow falls only on the background of your quilt, the couched line and its shadow will be parallel to each other. If the shadow runs into any obstacles, such as blocks, it has to go "up and over" them.

There are many great stamps available in craft stores and on the Internet.

STAMPING

Stamping is another way to create a drop shadow behind an image. There are many great stamps available in craft stores and on the Internet. For best results, stick to simple, easy-to-cut shapes for this technique.

You can use acid-free stamping ink or acrylic paint for stamping. The shadow color should be gray, black, or a darker, duller shade of the background color. The image color is up to you. The top image will be at a slight diagonal from the shadow in the direction of the light source. Don't twist the image though; keep the orientation the same.

1. First, stamp the image on the fabric—that is, the image that is casting the shadow.

2. Stamp the same image on a sheet of freezer paper and cut it out carefully. This will be the mask. Once the paint has dried, iron the freezer paper mask over the image on the fabric, lining them up so that the image is completely covered.

First stamp the image on the fabric.

Cover the image with a freezer paper mask.

3. Stamp the same image, a little below and off to one side, using shadow paint, in the opposite direction of the light source.

4. Remove the freezer paper mask.

Then stamp the shadow, off to one side.

The image is shadowed.

MARKERS

Fabric markers also can be used to create shadows. Adding a line with a gray marker along the edge of an appliquéd or fused object can create a subtle shadow. Markers can also be used to shadow couched yarns.

Markers come in a limited variety of colors, and unlike paints, they can't be mixed to make different colors. Be sure to test your marker on a scrap sample before marking on your quilt. Be forewarned that a black marker creates a very strong shadow. And some markers bleed into the fabric, leaving an unacceptably blotchy line.

Marking a shadow along a fused or appliquéd piece is easy. Just hold the marker with the tip flat to create a wide shadow. Be sure to shadow only the edges of the piece that require a shadow! Taper off the marker as you come to an unshadowed edge.

Aotearoa detail

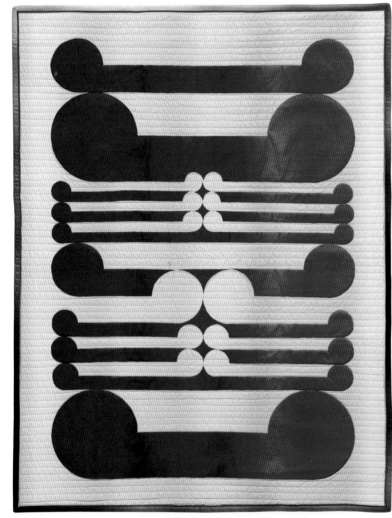

Aotearoa, 40" x 30". The edges of the shadow taper to nothing as they come around to an unshadowed edge.

Markers can also be used to shadow a line of couched yarn. The shadow should parallel the couching.

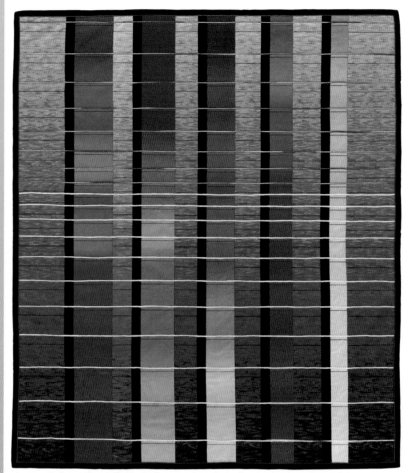

Aurora Lake, 40" x 35". Techniques: pieced shadows, shadowed couching.

Aurora Lake detail

ETCETERA

Other surface design techniques can also be used for shadowing. Anything that will mark on fabric will also have possibilities for adding shadows and depth. Think about using any or all of the following:

- Silk-screening
- Watercolor crayons or pencils
- Water-soluble oil pastels
- Thickened Procion dyes
- Foiling

These "minor tools" are often overlooked or unknown. Sometimes you need a minor tool to make a quilt. . .major!

Shallow, 40" x 48". Technique: silk-screened shadows.

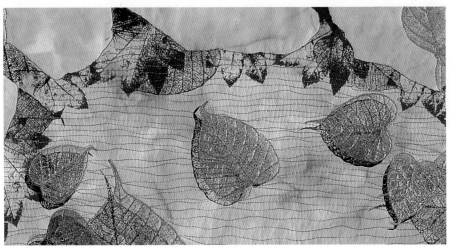

Shallow detail. Silk-screened foiled leaves float in a shallow puddle.

Use all the tools in your personal toolbox, especially those most important tools of all: the heart and mind of an artist.

I find that I can hardly limit myself to one technique when I am making a quilt. I may start out with a predominant technique—say, piecing—but somewhere along the line, I'll dip into my toolbox of quilting techniques for my oil paints, a little fusing, maybe some stamping, and finally I'll finish up with some special quilting. One of the hardest things for me to do is to make a quilt with only one technique. It's the blending of these techniques, the ability to draw out something unexpected as a piece develops, that excites me all along the way.

I hope that it will excite you too, as you make your way on this creative journey of quiltmaking. Use all the tools in your personal toolbox, especially those most important tools of all: the heart and mind of an artist.

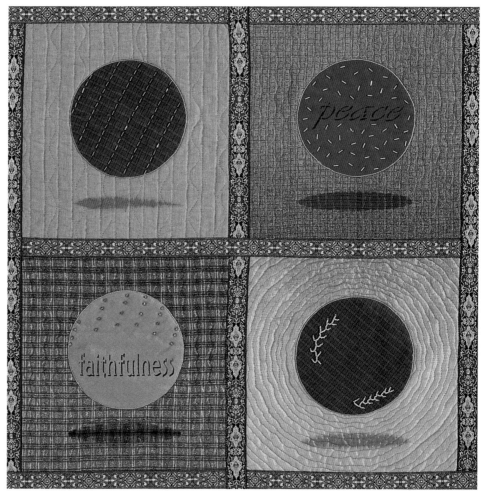

Fruits of the Spirit detail (full quilt page 97)

Gallery

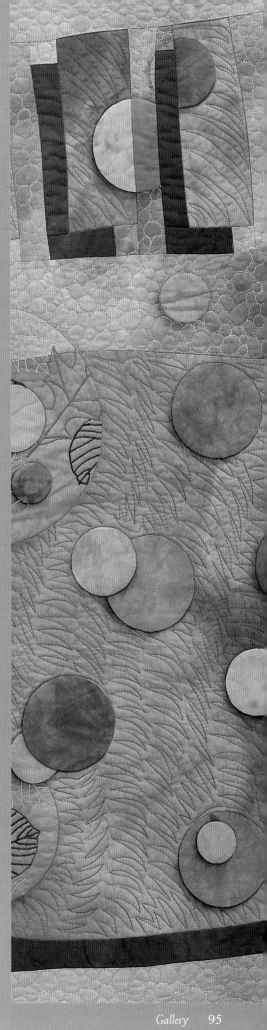

Botanica, 100" x 84"
Techniques: discharged shadows, perspective setting

Fruits of the Spirit, 63" x 48"
Techniques: discharged shadows, silk-screening

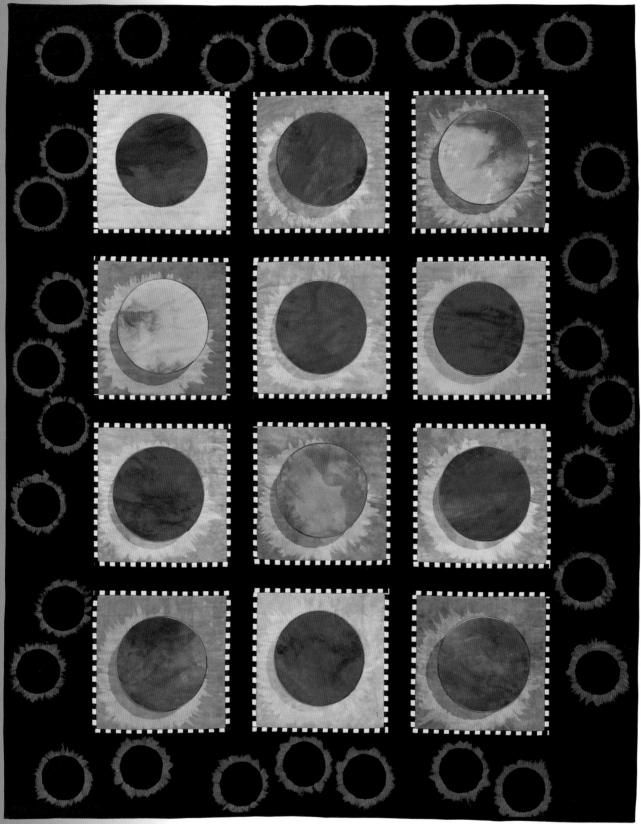

Corona, 52" x 43"
Technique: discharged shadows

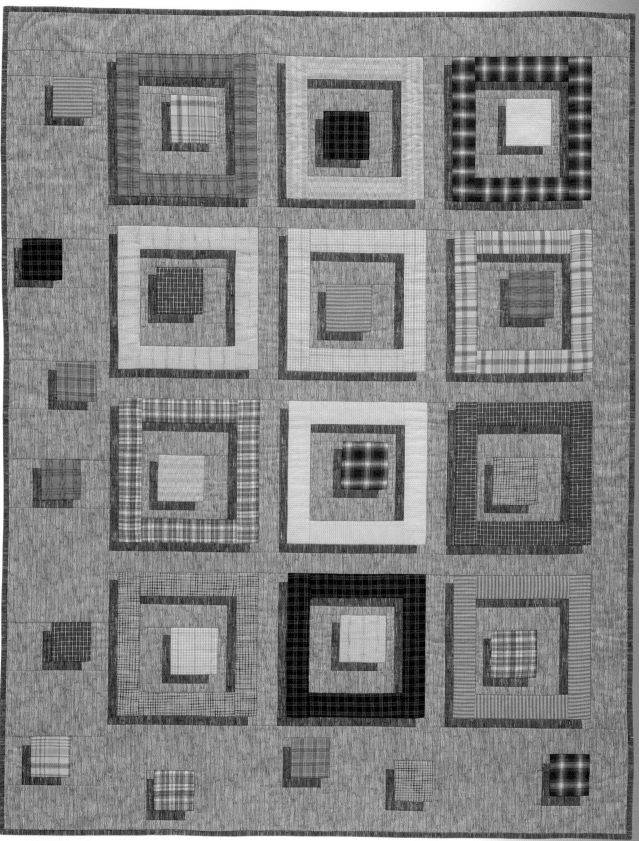

Cluster Class, 51" x 41"
Technique: pieced shadows

Equinox, 53" x 38"
Technique: pieced shadows

Three-Leaves Potholder
Techniques: appliquéd shadows, quilting

One-Leaf Potholder
Techniques: appliquéd shadows, quilting

Yosemite Triptych, 40" x 46"
Techniques: free-form piecing, shadowed appliqué, implied shapes

Family Monuments, 40" x 36"
Technique: pieced shadows

Solar Energy, 41" x 41"
Techniques: discharged shadows, pieced shadows

Happens Every Fall, 48" x 58"
Techniques: discharged shadows, implied shapes

The Butterfly Collection
by Colleen Wise and
Hannah Wise-Maas, 30" x 25"
Technique: fused sheer shadows

Enmeshed, 49" x 62"
Technique: pieced shadows

String of Pearls, 34" x 29"
Technique: discharged shadows

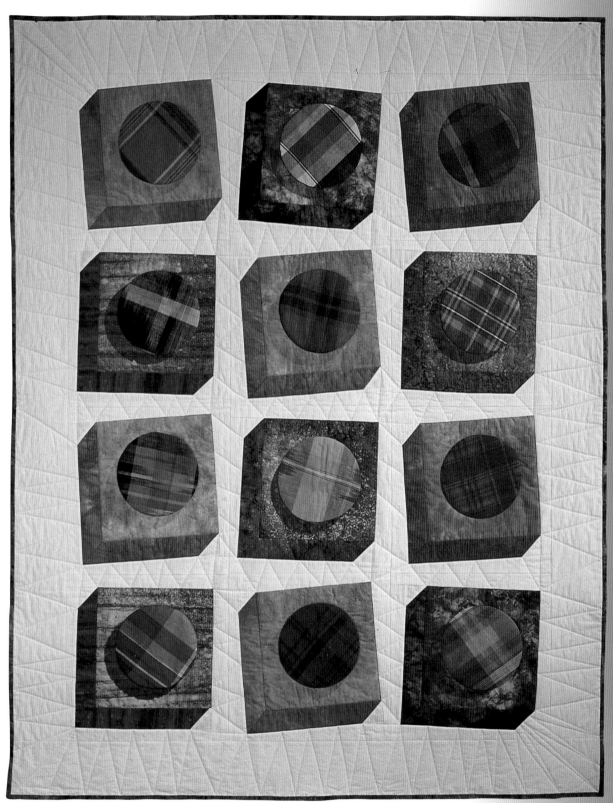

Stumbling Blocks, 50" x 38"
Techniques: discharged shadows, perspective setting

Narrows Bridge, 59" x 48"
Technique: pieced shadows

Also on 9/11, 62" x 58"
Techniques: discharged shadows, fusing

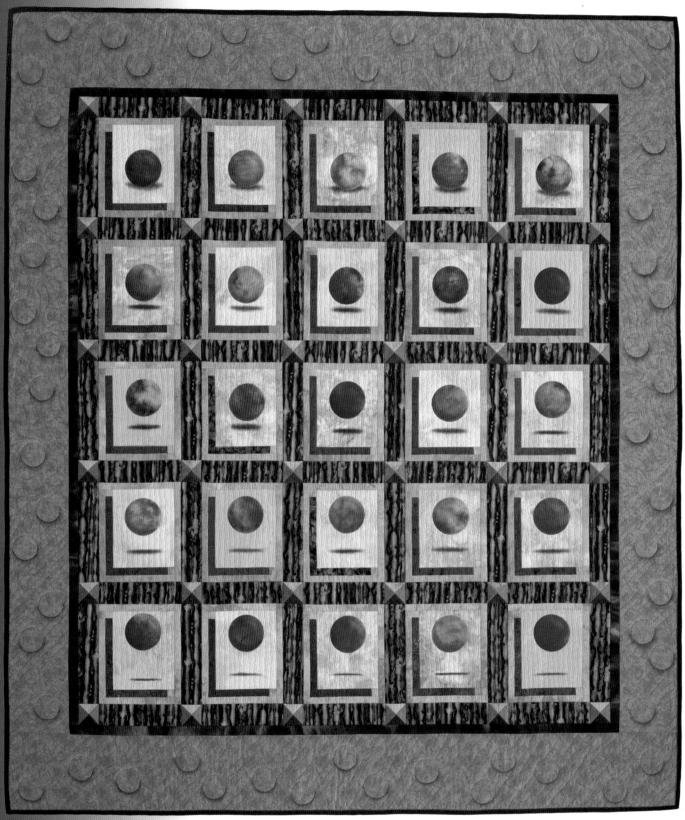

Gravity, 86" x 75".
Techniques: painted puddled shadows, painted embossed shapes.

RESOURCES

Hand-painted fabrics, patterns, and kits:

BARB'S ELEGANT DESIGNS
www.barbsed.com
Barb Sherrill
Graham, Washington
(253) 847-6039
barb@barbsed.com

Hand-dyed fabrics:

JUST IMAGINATION
www.justimagination.com
Judy Robertson
P.O. Box 583
Burlington, WA 98233
(360) 755-1611
judy@justimagination.com

Discharge, Anti-chlor, and dyeing supplies:

PRO CHEMICAL & DYE
www.prochemical.com
P.O. Box 14
Somerset, MA 02726
Orders: 1-800-2-BUY-DYE
Technical support: 508-676-3838
Fax: 508-676-3980
promail@prochemical.com

Stencils:

REVISIONS
www.revisions-ericson.com
Available at many local shops
Diane Ericson
1081 Avocado Road
Corralitos, CA 95076
dericson@redshift.com

INDEX

About the Author

Colleen's background is in science and engineering, and her quilts reflect that in their strong graphic quality. Creating designs and solving problems are her favorite parts of the process; cutting, sewing, and pressing are just the means to the end. She loves to play with illusions in her quilts, creating three dimensions on a two-dimensional surface. Her quilts have won prizes in national and international shows as well as being exhibited at Quilt National 2001. Colleen teaches, lectures, and exhibits her work throughout the United States and internationally.

Colleen has always enjoyed working with fiber. While in college and living overseas, she used to spin yarn and design her own hand-knitted sweaters. When her mother, Arlene Wise, introduced her to quilting in 1991, Colleen found a new passion. She started out as a traditional quilter but, after a few quilts, started creating her own original designs.

Colleen and her husband live in Puyallup, Washington, with their three children. Colleen stays busy volunteering in her children's schools, in Scouts, and in the community. In her spare time, she loves working in her perennial garden, traveling, reading, and hiking in the mountains.